UPHILL
ALL
THE
WAY

UPHILL ALL THE WAY

Edna
Jaques

Western Producer Prairie Books
Saskatoon, Saskatchewan

Cover designed by Warren Clark

Printed in Canada by
Modern Press
Saskatoon, Saskatchewan

Canadian Cataloguing in Publication Data

Jaques, Edna, 1891-
    Uphill all the way

ISBN 0-919306-86-1
1. Jaques, Edna, 1891-   — Biography.
2. Poets, Canadian (English) — Biography.
I. Title.
PS8519.A8A3   C811'.5'2   C77-002185-9
PR9199.3

Dedicated with love to my girls:
daughter—Helen Joyce
granddaughter—Nancy Ellen
granddaughter—Louise Anne

Contents

CHAPTER 1

The
Beginning

Evidently God thought this lifework of mine would take two to carry because he sent a pair of twin girls to make sure the job would be done. Edna and Erie were born one cold Saturday morning, the 17th of January, 1891, back there in the Gay Nineties when a doctor's fee for a baby was two dollars and a cup of tea. He really asked my father for four dollars at the time, seeing there were two babies. My dad split the difference and gave him three.

I, Edna Jaques, weighed exactly three and a quarter pounds; Erie Linton Jaques, the other twin, weighed less, and we were the skinniest, bluest looking kids ever born in Ontario. Even my good-hearted mother was ashamed of us and they say that dad took one horrified look at what he had produced and went out and got plastered (the one and only time of his life) in the old Globe Hotel in Collingwood.

But when he came home, sober and sorry for it, he laid the pair of us crossways on a pillow and walked the floor with us and wept and swore he would work his fingers to the bone to give us a chance and we'd never do a bit of work as long as we lived — never.

How wrong he was, how very wrong. For, from the day I was twelve and started to herd cattle, I've worked like a galley slave and it's been uphill all the way — very uphill — steep and rocky, with hard slugging. Although I wouldn't trade places with the queen, I wouldn't go back over the trail I've come for a million dollars in guinea gold.

But let's go back to the babies, my sister and me, back to the bottom of the hill. We were so tiny that my grandmother would take the ring off her fingers and slide it over our hands and up to our shoulders.

They made little canton flannel nightcaps for us that are now in the library in Collingwood. They wouldn't cover the head of a good-sized doll. Everyone in town came to see us. I've met old women who told me that the Sunday after we were born, the sidewalks were crowded with curious folk coming to see the Jaques twins.

How we managed to survive I'll never know, for there were no baby clinics in those days, no prepared food (only what Nature provided) and visitors rocked and bounced us, and poked their fingers into our ribs to satisfy themselves we were still alive. If we squirmed and squawled, we were still alive, and they went home shaking their heads and muttering into their beards.

After about six weeks of the unequal battle, my sister gave up, and with a sigh that shook her tiny frame (my mother said) she flew back to the heaven she had so lately left. Her little tombstone can still be seen in the Collingwood cemetery; it's overgrown with lichen and trailing moss, but her name stands out — Erie Linton Jaques — bright as the printing on a new copper. After that it was up to me to carry the banner for us both, although now and then I've envied her, her quiet grave and sinless death.

The day of the funeral everyone, even good Doctor Aylsworth, wanted them to wait a day or two until I died, so they could lay us both in the one tiny white coffin, but my grandfather shook his head and said, "No, this one will live." Lifting his eyes across the frozen garden, he added, "She'll see us all in our graves and bring honor to the name she bears."

How did they know — those old fellows — how did they know those strange hidden things.

CHAPTER 2

My
Ancestors

My father was the captain of a passenger ship sailing from Collingwood to Fort William, in the days when boats were big time.

The Jaques family came from Yorkshire over 100 years ago. They had been Huguenots living near Hazenbrook, France, up near the Belgium border and being of Protestant faith were in danger of their lives day and night. I can remember my grandmother telling us how a British battleship would be standing a few miles off shore and when night came, the sailors would come in lifeboats and find the frightened refugees hiding along the rocks and cliffs, bring them out to the big ships and take them to the safety of England.

So the Jaques family settled in Yorkshire and became sailors and masters of "brigs", as an old letter in the family Bible tells. There they lived until 1835, when they again pulled up stakes and came to Canada in a little sailing ship that was driven off the course. My grandfather, Benjamin Jaques, told us they were nearly a month on the perilous journey and half-starved by the time they landed. They finally settled near the village of Colborne, Ontario and got crown land, two miles south of number two highway as we know it now. The number of their land was Lot 20. Here they farmed and fished and starved. Others who came with them got land too and many of their descendants are there today, prosperous and happy with nice families.

At this corner on Highway 2 a little church stands. It was built in 1861 and was originally Methodist, but is now United. Of the thirteen people who contributed to the building fund, seven of them were the Jaques family. In the registry office at Colborne is the original crown grant for the land. One of the first trustees was Joseph Jaques.

No interior changes have been made in over 100 years; it's just been painted and cleaned. It was built without a basement. The outside walls are clapboard, painted white with narrow stained glass windows. The pews are the original ones, and the oak timbers were donated by Thomas Ventress, a brother of our great-grandmother, Mary Ventress. The pulpit was handmade and shows the marks of the adze and plane to this day.

At the right of the church lies the cemetery. Many of the stones bear the name of Jaques. The first one, John, died in 1850; beside him is the grave of his wife, Mary Ventress, and four small children.

John's son, Benjamin, was my grandfather. He married Ursula Linton. His son, Charles, was my father. He married Ellen Donohue of Waterdown, Ontario. They had six children: Bruce, Clyde, Edna and Erie, Madge and Arlie.

My grandfather was just a little boy when they came to Canada from Staithes, Yorkshire, England. Nearly 100 years after the first settlement I wrote of them:

MY ANCESTORS

I do not know their pedigree,
    Their breeding or their worth,
But this I know they gave to me
    A love of common earth,
The smell of furrows wide and clean
    A love of sun and rain,
Their gardens sweet with mignonette
    Will live in me again.

And someone nurtured by the sea,
    Who loved its wind and spray
Passed down across the years to me

The joy that's mine today.
For I can smell the salty breath
When quiet tides are low
Because some person living there
Had loved it long ago.

Because some unremembered soul
Was glad of firelight
I am content with little rooms
That shut me from the night,
And when I see the dawn come up
All stormy from the sea,
A thankful fisherman at dawn
Is glad again in me.

For songs that beat against my heart,
From some dim fountain fed
Were hers before she went to live
Among the quiet dead,
And all that's fine and good and clean,
The substance and the sum,
A part of all that went before
The seed of all to come.

But the lure of the sea was in them still, so they left
Colborne in 1879 for Collingwood, Ontario and again became
sailors. When dad was twenty-seven he secured his captain's
papers and from then on until 1902 he was captain of a
passenger boat sailing from Collingwood to Fort William, when
boats were big time. One of his boats, as I recall, was the
Britannic; another one was the *Northern Bell,* that burnt under
him one awful night. Dad, being the last one to leave the ship,
broke through the burning deck three times before grabbing the
rail and heaving himself overboard where a lifeboat was
waiting for him.

CHAPTER 3

My First Memory

My first real memory is of Christmas Day when I was five years old. We used to hang our stockings (two of them held together with a pin) on the back of a chair in the kitchen. Each one had his special chair; mine was near the dining room door. They told us that Santa Claus came down the chimney; as there was a huge coal-burning stove in that room, I figured I'd be the closest one when he landed and would get the most. Why I didn't figure that he would be burnt to a crisp if he came down and into the stove, I don't know, but that is where I hung my stockings.

How I wanted a little toy stove. I would ask my mother wistfully if she thought I would get one and she'd smile her kindly smile and say, "Maybe." Well, I got it. Running down in the dark on Christmas morning I made a beeline for my chair and there it was — a tiny iron stove, about eight inches square with little pots and pans to go with it, and a tiny teakettle. No gift I have ever received in my life gave me the pure joy that the little stove did. I took it to bed with me for weeks.

We always had Christmas dinner at noon at my grandfather's home, a little house on Cedar Street with two or three lean-tos on it, but cozy and warm with a stove in nearly every room; there was a woodshed at the back with a corner partitioned off for a toilet. How we loved to get out there and see the pictures that grandma had pasted on the walls: pretty girls, kids, dogs, flowers, plates of apples, and fat ladies in long dresses and floppy hats.

There was a well under the house with a pump in the kitchen, a huge iron thing that fascinated us. We used to make a beeline for it the minute we got into the house and start to pump. But if they saw or heard us coming, they tied the handle to the main pipe; how disappointed we would be if the pump was "tied".

At Christmas my grandmother would have a long table set in the dining room, which was two steps up from the kitchen. There was a bedroom at one end with the fattest, biggest feather tick I ever saw in my life. On it was a white spread. A little bureau and washstand stood in one corner and there were a couple of braided rugs on the floor.

At the other end of the dining room was a door that led into a tiny parlor where we hardly dared to go. We would tiptoe in, half-scared, as it was never opened except on Christmas Day. It had a queer musty smell that scared us to death and we never stayed long in there, I can tell you.

There was a big bay window in the dining room where grandma kept her flowers. I loved it, with the bright red geraniums and shamrocks and foliage plants with lovely leaves. All my life I have kept in my heart a picture of that window and wished I had one, but I never got it.

For me, the big event of Christmas Day was the moment grandma would come into the kitchen from the woodshed (where she had an extra cookstove). There was a little step and up she'd come carrying a huge platter with a golden brown turkey on it. Her face would be red as fire, but there was a sort of triumphant look on it, as if, for her too, this was the crowning event of the year.

There was always a good crowd of us: dad's brother, John, and his wife and three lovely daughters; Aunt Hattie and Uncle Gilford Pearsall; Byron, the youngest son; and our seven which included the two big brothers, myself and two little sisters.

Grandad would say grace, then the carving and passing dishes and laughter would start, everyone praising grandma's cooking, and enjoying pickles, jelly, beets, cranberry sauce, homemade catsup and mashed potatoes, with brown gravy dripping across the plates. For dessert we ate mince pie and plum pudding until we were stuffed to the gills and hardly able to walk away from the table.

The afternoon was spent with everyone talking and getting ready for supper, which would consist of cold turkey, rich home-canned fruit, Christmas cake and cookies.

About nine, maw would gather her little family up, wrap us in our warm coats and bonnets and scarves. Dad would carry the baby home, and all of us would walk in the middle of the road, loving the snow under our feet and the shine of the full moon; finally there would be the lovely opening of the door and settling into our warm beds.

CHAPTER 4

Precious
Days

I learned my ABC's from the damper of the cookstove in the kitchen. Cookstoves in those days were made of cast iron and burned hardwood. They had little platforms in front called dampers, with raised letters on them. (I suppose the letters referred to the name of the stove and where it was made.) So I copied them carefully and that shiny warm damper was my first blackboard. I imagine the family supplied the missing letters of the alphabet. I had a slate bound with red felt and a pencil wrapped in blue and red striped paper; with these I made my bow into the world of letters that I have found so rewarding and full of grace.

I started school when I was seven, at the old Central School in Collingwood. It would be nice to say that I loved it, but unfortunately I didn't. As a matter of fact, most of it was over my head. I just couldn't see any sense in figures. They danced before my eyes like puppets on a string. But the stories and poems, ah they were different. I knew all the poems in the book by heart long before the other kids. I sang them to little tunes as I went along, wept over them and sounded out the words, one at a time, like a nun telling her beads. Words, just plain ordinary words, they were always such precious things to me.

I think I began to write poetry about that time. I was ashamed of it, or maybe I was just being afraid of being laughed at, so I hid the poems in little nooks and corners, taking them out now and then when I was alone, making them "nicer", I used to say.

The next five years were probably the happiest years of my life. We had a lovely home on Fourth Street and a loving mother; our father, who was away all summer on his boat, came home now and then and brought us toys that the Indians gave him (probably for free rides on the freight deck of his boat). He also brought baskets of blueberries and freshly caught fish. We always had a feast the day dad came home.

We had nice friendly neighbors too. There was Mrs. Hammil, who lived in the next block; Mrs. White, who lived on Maple Street; the Telfer girls and their brother next door, who let us pick apples from their tree; Mrs. Swiggley across the street, a big laughing woman; and Mrs. Trott, who lived on the corner. They would come and sit on the front steps of a summer evening and talk and laugh, and we would play with their kids. Everyone would leave about nine o'clock and go home to bed. There were no card games or drinking or husband stealing, just happy neighbors, and as far as we knew, no special problems.

We played with their children — Dorothy Hammil (we are still friends when we meet in Victoria after eighty years); Josie White, who died young; Jessie Davidson; and the two Bruce girls who lived on Beech Street. I had tea in their old home last summer (the preacher lives there now) and I could hardly drink my tea for seeing them peeping from the corners of the room, or shyly laughing from the hall door.

We had no special entertainment, I can tell you. We played with our dolls, dug holes in our back yards, walked fences (those old wooden ones), climbed the trees, went to the little creek near grandma's to wade and chase minnows, bare-footed most of the time and happy as kids are supposed to be.

Nine o'clock was bedtime; my sister and I slept in a little wooden cot in my mother's room, as I was a nervous child and couldn't sleep without the comfort of my mother near-by.

Most of our social life was centered around the old Methodist church on Maple Street. For Sunday school on Sunday morning, Madge and I would be dressed up in stiff white dresses with short socks and white slippers. How we loved walking up the quiet lovely street, going in the side door and upstairs where the kindergarten room was, getting little leaflets with pictures of Jesus blessing the children, the white square buildings of Jerusalem and men with flowing robes and white turbans on their heads held on with circles of red or black ribbon.

I remember an elderly lady who taught us, who was frankly stout and wore a basque and skirt. The basque had a row of buttons up the front and looked as if it would burst open any minute. But she had a nice face, rosy cheeks, a happy smile and the buttons held.

The Christmas concert was the highlight of the year. There would be a Christmas tree with presents on it for everyone, a short program with parents beaming out there in the semi-darkness of the church, kids panting up the stairs, tripping over their long skirts, forgetting their "pieces" and being a little afraid of Santa Claus.

I remember my sister Madge, singing a song, sort of sitting down on the platform, rocking her doll in my yellow doll cradle. The harder she sang, the harder she rocked the cradle, and the doll flopped wildly from side to side. My mother laughed so hard at her that dad got kind of mad and told her to shut up, but she kept right on and enjoyed every minute of it.

There were sleigh rides in the winter. Collingwood is noted for a lot of snow, and how we enjoyed riding down the hills on the edge of town, coming home in the gentle dusk caked with snow and hungry as bears. How good our supper tasted, how cozy and warm the kitchen was with dad smoking his pipe in a big red arm chair and reading the paper.

One winter afternoon, too cold to be outside, I was sitting on the floor in the kitchen when the first "flash" of poetry came to me. I had been copying the printing of the letters that were on the damper of the stove, on a slate, when suddenly words began forming together, like the tiny verses on the Sunday school leaflets, words that kind of sang together, making music, telling a story.

I didn't know they called it poetry, I only knew it sounded nice and after that, now and then the flash would come, like the echo of a voice singing somewhere, or something you kind of remembered.

When I was about nine, two lady evangelists by the name of the Misses Hall came to the church and were holding meetings every night which I attended. I suppose someone came with me. After listening to their powerful words, they invited the congregation to come forward and pledge their love and loyalty to God, and be saved. Being young, I was likely carried away with their stories of love and protection and as the crowd moved up the aisle toward the front, I joined them, and stood in the front row as they came along and spoke to each one quietly as if answering a special need for help.

When one of them got to me, she leaned down and whispered, "God will protect you wherever you go or whatever you do, if you will only trust Him." After that I crept quietly back to my seat, and went home.

She never knew what she did. For in all the turbulent years that followed — through danger, poverty, being homeless, out of work, out of money, in big cities or on the homestead, on planes or ships at sea, in situations that would make your hair stand on end, those comforting words would come to me, clear as a bell, word for word as she said them, "God will take care of you. . . ." Just saying them would take the fear away; the loneliness would go and my heart would be at peace.

CHAPTER 5

Dad's Decision

Late in the fall of 1901, dad was coming down from Fort William on his boat with a full load of passengers and loaded to the gunwales with heavy freight on the lower decks. It was to be the last trip of the season as navigation closes early in November or late October, depending on the weather and storms.

All went well until they got out in the middle of Lake Superior; then the blow fell. A terrible storm blew up with winds of almost hurricane force. The stout little ship battled bravely with waves that threatened to swamp her at any minute.

For three days and three terrible nights they fought and prayed and hoped, and by the end of the third day, dad finally steered her into the dock at Collingwood, more dead than alive.

Everything on the outside of the boat was gone — lifeboats, life rafts, railings; windows were smashed, even half of the smoke stack was gone, cut in two by the pounding waves. There was dad on the little look-out at the front of the boat, exhausted and sick, but holding grimly to the wheel, and sort of triumphant.

The crew were all in their bunks below, sick as dogs; only the first mate was left, standing grimly beside dad as they limped into the dock, more dead than alive, and about sixty passengers, sick and frightened but also thankful to be alive.

Dad used to tell how, one by one, they passed before him and the first mate, shook hands with them and thanked him for bringing them home alive. He used to tell about the half-dozen ships that never made it; they just capsized and went to the bottom, with everyone and everything on board, lost.

But out there in the wild beating of the storm, dad shook his fist at God (up there in the heavens) and vowed that if he ever got his two feet on dry ground he'd stay there and never go sailing again, and he never did.

Lake Superior is a beautiful lake. They claim it's the largest fresh water lake in the world, and although she is a terrible mistress when riled, sailors still love the wide expanse of sparkling water that stretches like a sea from horizon to horizon and the eerie lights that dance on the water on moonlit nights breaking your heart with their beauty.

Dad had a cousin who farmed near Yellowgrass, after selling his farm just outside of Collingwood in the Blue Mountains. His name was Robert Jaques. He came to visit dad one day in January, 1902. They were in the parlor talking and laughing together, my mother and us little girls were in the dining room where maw was reading and us kids were playing school. Suddenly the folding doors between the two rooms opened and dad stood in the doorway (I can see him yet) and loudly announced to my mother, "We're leaving Collingwood." Taking a long breath he said, "We're going homesteading in the North West Territories. . . ." (as Saskatchewan was then called).

My mother fainted. She could faint more quickly than anyone I ever knew. Dad picked her up and laid her on the couch, and poured water on her face until she came to. She staggered into the kitchen and started getting supper, still white as a sheet, crying between bites. She hustled us off to bed right after supper, but in the morning, dad was still excited and talking a blue streak, trying to make her see what a wonderful place the prairies were, with a million acres of good land, the best in the world, and a man could get 160 acres without paying a cent for it.

Then the preparations for leaving were started. They sold the lovely house to a Mr. Carey for $2500.

After that, everything went, lock, stock and barrel: furniture, carpets, knickknacks, my brothers' bicycle, even our doll carriages, and my mother's pride and joy, the piano.

But they took a few things, including two wooden veranda rocking chairs. It would be fifteen years before they had a veranda to rock on, but they went anyway, with a half-dozen trunks, five huge packing boxes of dishes, and last but not least, a huge red book with fiery gold letters on it and the letters said, "Remedies for Man and Beast". It had terrifying pictures in it of sick and dead people and stiff dead horses.

That book was to make history. As we lived twenty-five miles from town (Moose Jaw), where you had to go in a lumber wagon with a team of plow horses to get a doctor, that book was cherished like the ark of the covenant. Wherever we went or whatever was lost, strayed or stolen, that precious book was kept safe on the top shelf of the pantry for over fifty years, its pages frayed and worn, leafed over by day and night and believed in like the Ten Commandments.

If a horse got sick, down came the book, its red cover making a bright spot on the kitchen table, with the coal oil lamp and maw's glasses. Dad would turn to the page where it said, "Cure for colic in horses" and my mother would start to haul down bottles, and a cup for measuring.

What they put into it, I never knew, but it fizzed and burped and shot water to the ceiling, no matter how hard dad pressed his finger on the top.

What it did to the horse I do not know, but from the squealing and stamping and cussing and the "whoas" that came from the barn, we knew the horse was either strangling or swallowing the stuff and dad would come in, wet to the elbows, and kind of white around the gills.

If a kid got sick, the procedure was about the same. The book was brought down and read frantically. I remember once I had neuralgia or some awful kind of pain in my head. So dad read aloud, "If there is extreme pain in a child's head, give it a Sterns headache wafer and the pain will immediately subside." They gave me two big ones the size of a quarter. The outside kind of melted when it was swallowed with a glass of water, or it would have stuck in your gullet and killed you.

About five minutes after I got the pills down, I started to get sleepy. My head went fuzzy and I went into a stupor; my legs buckled under me and I went down in a heap in the yard. Everyone was scared to death.

I could hear my mother's voice from far away screaming, "Make her walk, make her walk!" So they heaved and pulled on me and got me moving and for two hours by the clock, the family took turns walking me. I can remember it distinctly; every time I threatened to fold up and go to sleep, someone would yell, "Make her walk, keep her going," and from some unknown inner strength I'd walk, supported on each side by two people urging me on.

Then, after making me drink about a quart of water, they decided I was cured and let me sleep and I never came to until noon the next day. But the pain was gone and I never mentioned it again; I can tell you if I had a pain I kept it to myself.

For us, the three little girls, a mustard plaster was the favorite cure-all. They were put on us wherever a pain was felt. I had a backache once and maw got out the mustard. You were supposed to mix it half-and-half with flour and the white of an egg to keep it from blistering. Being wintertime, there were no eggs, so she just mixed it with water and clapped it on the small of my back.

As soon as the warmth of the plaster eased the pain, I dropped off to sleep and slept for three hours. When I woke I was in agony from the burning, so maw took the plaster off, carefully I must say, but a patch of skin about four-by-five inches came with it. That finished me with mustard plasters.

Another cure was salt pork with lots of pepper and salt on it. As I so often had a sore throat, I wore a perpetual collar of salt pork around my neck from fall until spring. I don't suppose it hurt me, but I must have smelled like an old pork barrel most of the time and I never really got the pepper out of my pores until spring.

Nothing escaped the book: pigs, cows, hens, dogs, cats and kids. Everyone that breathed on the place came in for a dose some time, whether they needed it or not.

New homesteaders coming into the country often would be

sick from the alkali water and would come to dad for help. The book would be brought down. Dad would run his finger down the index and when he figured out what ailed the man who had come for help, he'd stop, and maw would mix up a dose that would curl you hair and the man would gulp it down with tears running down his cheeks, thank dad, and go home.

He never really killed anyone, but I know of two or three men who never spoke to him as long as they lived, after what they had suffered from his hands.

CHAPTER 6

Moose
Jaw

In the meantime, the preparations for leaving Collingwood went on. My mother got in a dressmaker at fifty cents a day, and she made new dresses for us. Madge and I got blue sailor suits with pleated skirts, middy blouses, trimmed with rows of white braid on the collars and long sleeves, and Sunday dresses of soft rose-colored material that I thought were the prettiest dresses in the world.

She also had a couple made for herself, dark stiff dresses with flowing skirts that almost touched the floor, and a couple of blouses that we called "waists" with long sleeves and lace on the cuffs.

Dad bought a long coon-skin coat for himself. I remember he paid thirty-five dollars for it and maw told him he paid far too much.

He also bought her a short black fur coat that looked like dog hair with a kind of ruffle of fur at the back. It came just below her hips, which proved a poor coat for warmth, as it didn't come down far enough to keep her warm. I think the dog eventually inherited it. It lay behind the stove, and looking back, I think the dog was the most comfortable one in that little homestead house, where the nail heads were covered with frost in the wintertime and crackled like pistol shots in the middle of the night.

Soon the fatal day of leaving came. We drove to the station in Smalley's cab, which thrilled us to death. Never before or since have we ridden in a cab. My mother held the littlest one on her lap, and as she looked back, the tears rolled down her cheeks. She had loved her home and been so proud of it, and now she was leaving it forever.

How were we to know, any of us, that never again would we have such a lovely home, in such a quiet street in one of Ontario's loveliest towns, with neighbors next door to run in and out and have a little happy gossip, with a school two blocks away and a quiet church down Maple Street, where God seemed so near and reliable and people we knew and liked always within call.

We left Collingwood in February, 1902. When we got to the station we found that most of our little friends had come down to see us off. They were laughing and chasing each other around the platform of the station, kissing us goodbye, and wishing they were going with us.

Grandpa Jaques came down too, shivering in the gray dawn, kissing every kid he saw. He was too far gone to distinguish between us and everyone else. I can see him wiping the tears away and staring up the track with his long white beard blowing in the cold winter dawn.

We boarded the train with shrieks and goodbyes. Then there was a sharp whistle and we started to move, waving until we were half-a-mile away, when we started to settle down and put our dolls to sleep and watch the other passengers.

We changed trains at Barrie; there was a great hustle and bustle around us; we had suitcases and extra coats, buffalo robes and shawls. My mother stared straight ahead and for once in his life dad left her alone; he just sat beside her and looked out the window.

We watched the trees flashing by on our way to North Bay and then we saw the rocky shores of Lake Superior, the vast expanse, frozen solid, mile after endless mile of stillness with absolutely no sign of life or humanity.

Dad pointed out to us the long island called the "Sleeping Giant" near Fort William and I can remember his face, after all these years, looking white, with a tear trickling down his cheeks as he (I am sure) bid goodbye to the waters. He had truly loved his boats and he knew that he would never walk the deck of a ship again as a captain, or chart his course between the half-hidden rocks and islands of the Great Lakes.

We rode in a tourist car with a little kitchen at one end where we could make a cup of tea or warm up meat and other food maw had packed in a little straw suitcase marked "grub".

How we enjoyed it, a picnic every day.

At night the red plush seats were turned over to make a bed with an "upper" that pulled down, where Madge and I slept like logs with the baby wedged in against the back, so she wouldn't fall out.

We were three days and nights getting to Moose Jaw, our destination. Dad's brother, Byron, had gone west at seventeen years of age to work on the C.P.R. railroad at Crow's Nest Pass. He had arrived in Moose Jaw with seventy-five cents in his pocket, a little fair boy, looking for work. He paid twenty-five cents for his supper, another quarter for a bed and the last twenty-five cents went for his breakfast. That very day he got a job and was shipped west and worked for a year in the mountains, as the steel moved farther west, linking the East to the West like a golden chain of people and land that will last, I hope, as long as the earth turns, and the stars sing together.

When his railroad work was done, Byron came back to Moose Jaw, took up a homestead ten miles north and one mile west of the town (or village as it was then). He built a little shack about twelve-by-sixteen and bought a team of horses, a walking plow, and proceeded to carve a home out of the wilderness of no man's land. Fifty years later he died rich, having gone back to Collingwood to retire with his wife who had also come from there. They had no children.

We arrived in Moose Jaw one cold bitter evening in March and went to a hotel for the night. In the morning Byron came for us with his team and a sleigh, amid hellos and laughter, for he was truly glad to see some of his own again.

We drove out to his homestead in the sleigh with old quilts, horse blankets and buffalo robes; we kids screamed in the back as the snow flew and the runners creaked in the little trail that wound across the trackless miles of snow.

His shack was smaller than anything we had ever seen,

with a homemade bunk at one end, and some cleats nailed on the wall to hold up a couple of shelves for his bits of dishes.

He burned wood, bringing it from Buffalo Lake — a few miles north of him. The newly-cut wood drying behind the stove made a fragrant smell in the air, like nothing else on earth.

My parents slept in the homemade bunk; the kids slept on the floor on a mattress. We thought it was fun and slept like young puppies curled around each other for warmth and, I suppose, a feeling of security.

CHAPTER 7

Our
Homestead

Dad and Bruce and Byron went to look for a homestead for us. Why they would drive twenty-five miles southeast of Moose Jaw to look for land is beyond me, as there must have been many homesteads they could have got nearer the town.

About twenty miles out they came to a house on the bank of the Moose Jaw Creek, where people by the name of Coventry lived. There were three brothers who had all come out to haul freight at the time of the Riel Rebellion and after that, got homesteads. Across the creek a little rickety bridge was built; strangely enough it stood up for years, to everyone's surprise, but it served the purpose and we used to shiver crossing it for it swayed and creaked, and dad always gave a sigh of relief after he got over it.

Francis Coventry was the kindest man I ever knew. He would help anyone who was in trouble of any kind, and would sell you stuff without robbing you. Forty years after, I put him into a poem which would surprise him I am sure. It is called "Old Rancher". He had a ranch at the Dirt Hills and a farm along the creek and he used to ride between the two places — about twenty miles on horseback — and often stopped midway to visit us and have a meal. Here is his poem:

OLD RANCHER

He makes his lonely fire of buffalo chips
    Beside a little stone rimmed water hole,
Eases the saddle on his patient horse,
    Then tethers him upon a sunny knoll,
Brews his strong tea in an old blackened pot
    Then sips it from a tin cup piping hot.

Old buffalo bones lie bleaching in the sun,
    A bit of broken hoof . . . a crumpled horn,
A rutted path skirting the coulee's rim
    A buffalo wallow deep and crudely worn,
A little patch of gleaming alkali
    Shimmering against the deep blue of the sky.

He slings his lariat with careless ease
    Fastening it loosely to the saddle thong,
Takes up the reins . . . digs in his shiny spurs
    Whistling a gay tune as he jogs along,
Sensing far off . . . an eager band
    Of settlers coming in to claim the land.

His wife made the best bread I ever tasted in my life. She baked it in huge round pans and would hold the loaf in the crook of her arm to cut it, slash butter on it and hand it to a hungry kid with a lovely smile. That is how I remember her to this day, with a loaf of bread under her arm, slashing off a slice and handing it to someone.

I think Mr. Coventry must have gone with dad to help him find the homestead. He pointed out that some day a road would be right along the front of it. How he knew, I'll never know, but there the road is to this day, straight as a die, running twelve miles due west of Rouleau to the dear knows where, about a hundred feet from the house.

They managed to find a corner stake buried in the long prairie wool and snow, tied a piece of shirt tail on it so they could find it again, as there wasn't a house or a shack within

23

miles of it. The number of our homestead was N.E. ¼-22-14-24.

Dad went back to Moose Jaw and filed on it on March 17, 1902. Surely St. Patrick himself must have leaned out the windows of heaven that golden top-of-the-morning and laid his blessing on it, for never was there a more beautiful summer than the one that followed, warm and still and filled with wonder for all of us.

How could my father know that bright St. Patrick's day that he too was making history. After his name on the homestead paper would come other names and other home-steaders. Men from every corner of the world would follow him, some on horseback, some walking with a poke over their shoulders, some in buggies, and democrats and wagons — new green ones with creaking wheels and swaying spring seats.

My oldest brother, Bruce, was only seventeen at that time, not old enough to take a homestead; you had to be eighteen. However, he got one later. My older brother, Clyde, never did get one. By the time he was eighteen the homesteads were all gone; that is how fast they went.

After they got back to Uncle Byron's, they drove in to Moose Jaw to buy horses. A carload of wild unbroken broncos had just been brought in from Montana; they were in a new corral near the station, wild-eyed, frightened, trying in vain to jump over the corral fence, snorting and pawing the ground, kicking each other, rearing up on their hind legs, frantic with fear.

Dad bought four of them. How they ever got the harnesses on them, I'll never know. He also bought a new sleigh and went back to Byron's where my mother and the kids had been while the men were away.

Dad had a couple of cousins living near Yellow Grass. He got in touch with them and they drove up to the homestead to help dad build a barn. A barn had to come first, in order to take care of the horses, as there were no fences or anything to shut them in, or keep them from getting away. If that happened everything was lost before they started.

The men slept under the sleigh on top of the snow until the barn was built; in spite of that crude shelter, not one of them even caught a cold. They were young and strong and filled with the excitement of doing something new and adventurous, I suppose. The barn was built sturdy and strong and lasted for over fifty years. It was new and shiny when we got there and ready for business.

So, one morning they came back, loaded us up and headed for the homestead thirty-five miles away. The whole trip is kind of hazy to me. I think we slept most of the way, arriving at dusk at the new barn, lonely and remote in that vast stillness, with coyotes howling at the new intruders and night coming down.

They had partitioned off a little corner in the barn like a box stall, set up the cookstove, thrown a couple of mattresses on the frozen ground, and there we lived for about three weeks until they could get the house built. I don't remember any discomfort or cold — many homesteaders did the same thing.

Although I had been writing little verses ever since I was seven or so, it was in that box stall that I first found the courage to recite one to my mother and was surprised that she thought it was good. Here is the poem as I remember it:

> The barn is nice, I love the way
> > You kind of smell the new-mown hay,
> I like to see the horses sleep
> > The lovely way the shadows creep
> Along the stanchions in the floor
> > And go out by the stable door.
>
> I like to have my mother near,
> > For then I have no creepy fear
> For sometimes in the dead of night
> > When there is only lantern light
> A kid gets frightened of it all
> > In the half-darkness of the stall.
>
> I must not give way to fears
> For Mother says we're pioneers.

In a stall next to ours, we could hear Bruce and Clyde, and the two cousins, snickering and laughing together; they slept on straw and horse blankets, safe and warm and strangely content in their rude shelter, evidently enjoying themselves.

The lantern hung on a four inch nail, driven into the two-by-four of the partition and I remember the lovely golden light it cast over us all, and the shadowy darkness where the broncos slept too (poor wild things); the smell of straw, new lumber and the virgin earth mingled together to give us untroubled sleep.

It took them about two weeks to get the house ready. They dug a little cellar, with board walls halfway up, and I remember the cold smell of the earth and the little creeping things that quickly dug their way back into the earth as we disturbed the tiny realm that had been theirs since the beginning of time. There were little lizards, snails, worms, tiny snakes and dozens of creeping things that we had never seen or thought of. The prairies, they say, had once been a vast inland sea; maybe these creatures had been left and as the waters receded, they just dug farther and farther down and became earth creatures again living from the land.

We moved one windy cold day in March, carrying the stuff from the barn to the new house, hardly finished yet, but better than the box stall.

The house was fourteen-by-twenty feet with a little attic above it. About six feet was partitioned off at one end for a bedroom where my parents slept. It had a window facing east, and a corner for maw's bureau, with nails hammered in under the stairs for their clothes.

There were two steps of the stairs in the kitchen and they became our favorite seat; we could get out of the way of everyone, and yet see what was going on. The steps sort of wound up to the upstairs; the roof was so low that anyone getting too close would bang his head.

At the west end my brothers slept on straw ticks with lots of blankets. We three little girls slept in the east end. It was partitioned off by a gray blanket at first. It too had a fat straw tick and warm flannelette blankets, with wool blankets on top; I never remember being cold, as long as I stayed in bed. In the morning our hair would be white with frost, and our noses red but we didn't mind. Our parents were young and had not learned bitterness (as they did twenty years later when the drought hit and everyone was poor) after working so hard all their lives.

Those straw ticks were very comfortable, and we used them for years. After threshing, my mother and I would take them out to the yard, near a new straw stack, and shake the old straw out of them. Then we'd stuff the lovely new sweet-smelling straw into them. Oat straw was best, as it didn't mat or lump. We'd put them back on the beds and I remember still the lovely golden smell of them, as if we had brought some of the quiet prairie in with them — and our dreams were sweet.

Later on, when we got real mattresses, I hated them. They were hard and had no smell. I rebelled and wanted to go back to the lovely straw ticks, but maw would have nothing to do with them; she said they made dirt and she had enough to do without sweeping up straw every day.

CHAPTER 8

Our First
Neighbor

Our first neighbors were Mr. and Mrs. William Gallaugher and their two little boys. I remember the day they came to the country. As we were the first settlers, all roads eventually led to our place; it later became the center of the settlement, like the hub of a wheel.

Mr. Gallaugher's brother lived north of Moose Jaw, at Caron. They had been living with him until they could get their bits of goods together and they drove from there to our place; it was about forty miles, a long day's journey with a team of horses and a wagon with a cow tied behind, a few hens in a slatted crate, some groceries and a few pieces of furniture.

Mr. Gallaugher had been out and filed on his homestead, and then went back for his family. Their place was about a mile-and-a-half south of us.

They had started out at dawn; it was June, and the mosquitoes were in their prime and that meant plain hell on earth. All that terrible day, from dawn to nearly dark, they fought the mosquitoes and great stinging flies and heat and homesickness and tears. Hour after hour the horses plodded on; the cow followed, oh so slowly, as the swaying wagon creaked and groaned.

All day long the mother sought to protect her children from the mosquitoes, until her own face and neck and hands and legs were solid masses of burning bites. I think she cried most of the time.

About seven in the evening they arrived at our little homestead shack; Mrs. Gallaugher was hysterical. The children had cried themselves out and were asleep; the father was almost in tears himself.

My mother went out and brought them into the house, comforting her the best she could. She set us younger children to bathing the boys' hands and faces and little burning legs with soda and water, patting the mixture on with a soft cloth while she comforted the mother and made her a cup of tea and washed her wounds.

That was the beginning of a friendship that never waned or grew stale, a friendship that sweetened the early years like molasses on bread; it never faded until the sod was laid above my parents' heads.

I can remember Mr. Gallaugher, who, years after, got some strange disease, and knew he was dying. He sent for dad to bid him goodbye and thank him for being so good to them all those years. I went with dad up the tiny stairs of their home. Mr. Gallaugher was sitting up in bed in a striped flannelette nightgown, holding his head and telling dad how it hurt. He looked like a little boy, kind of bewildered, crying a bit and bidding us goodbye. He died the next day and we were glad his pain was gone; I know his bed in heaven will be easy, for as far as anyone could know he led a blameless life, with a firm belief in the hereafter and God sitting on a white throne.

After the Gallaughers, other homesteaders began to come in. Hardly a day passed without a wagon load of them coming across the trackless miles, headed for our place, as it was the only house in all that vast emptiness. The homesteaders were always a welcome sight. Every family meant another neighbor and we sure needed people, if it was ever to be a good country to live in.

I think many of them just filed on their land in the land office in Moose Jaw, without seeing it first, and hoped for the best. Maybe they had relatives in Moose Jaw who had encouraged them to come west. Or maybe they had read glowing accounts in the Eastern papers about the "golden west" and as many of them had been living on rented farms in the East, or on "home farms" which couldn't support any more sons or daughters, they just pulled out and headed west. In our district, many of them were from Ontario, so we felt at home with them. But all in all, we had a good variety too.

Two miles east of us, two young boys by the name of Bailey got a homestead. They were "Barnardo" orphans from London, England. Arthur, the oldest, was a huge husky young man; the younger one, John, was small and frail and looked as if he had never had enough to eat. The way Arthur looked after his younger brother was heart-warming to see. He took the heavy end of every burden, lifting heavy wagon boxes and hayracks, building the hay stacks, hauling out the manure. They had a team of thin, sad-looking horses, and good old Arthur was always there, taking the heavy end of everything.

The Wyatt family came from the Ozarks. He was a huge man with a tiny wife, a son and two little girls. They came from Missouri and managed somehow to get a carload of settlers' effects: a team of horses, a broken-down wagon, a couple of cows, a pig and a half-dozen hens. They were hillbilly folk from the Ozark mountains and could sing anything you ever heard of. The father's voice was rich and powerful, while the girls' voices were sweet and full of pathos. I can hear them yet, singing "On the Banks of the Wabash Far Away," and "Billy Boy" and "Ridin' the Old Mule to Town".

A cousin near Drinkwater helped them get out to the homestead and then sort of abandoned them, as they were shabby and poor and no asset to the pride of the uncle or cousin, whichever it was.

I can remember them later on in the little schoolhouse which would be filled with mothers and fathers and rosy-cheeked children, well-fed, happy and content in a way that modern children don't know anything about.

The Hillsons were from Ontario, a father and mother, four sons and a pretty daughter, nice cheerful people. Mable used to ride a little Indian pony whose name was Flossie. She was half-wild and how Mable stayed on her back when Flossie took one of her bucking spells was more than anyone could figure. I saw Mable once, when Flossie had one of her bad moments, bucking like a steer, head down, tail flashing, wild-eyed.

We held our breath as Mable flopped back and forth —

her hat gone, her hair in her eyes, but she managed to stay on. Eventually Flossie tired and came meekly to the hitching post in our yard while Mable came into the house, pulled herself and clothes together, ate a couple of cookies and went home on Flossie.

Frasers came, father, mother and a little girl about my age called Kitty. Mrs. Fraser used to take in sewing to help their finances. She made most of our dresses until her eyes gave out. She would come to the house, bringing her little girl with her and sew and laugh and visit.

My mother always loved her, and the daughter, now nearly eighty, is still one of my best friends. I visited her the summer of 1975 at Qu'Appelle and we nearly laughed ourselves sick, recalling the old times.

Mrs. Fraser was the first "outsider" I ever showed my poetry. I had to sleep with her when she was sewing for us, and one night, just before we went to bed, I got up enough courage to show her my latest poem. Sitting there on the side of the bed I read it to her. She gave me a queer look and then said quietly, "Edna, that is beautiful. Are you sure you didn't copy that from a book?" I assured her I hadn't and she shook her head and said, "Well dear, you just keep on writing nice poems like that and maybe some day, you can get a book out." And with that for encouragement I took fresh heart and wrote many more which are lost now, but if my mother and Mrs. Fraser thought they were nice I was happy for weeks.

I could never understand how my mother, smart as she was, could hardly hold a needle in her hand; she was actually afraid of the old sewing machine. The only thing I ever saw her make was a pair of pants out of two flour sacks. It was Robin Hood Flour and on the front of the bag was a brown prairie chicken. My mother was always full of fun, so one day when a couple of neighbors were visiting she said to the two women, "Would you like to see my prairie chickens?". They said, "Sure," and up came her skirts and she showed them her pants with the two brown chickens. I'll never forget how they laughed and how embarrassed I was.

West Davey had been a hired man in Ontario. He got his

homestead and I'll never forget how proud and happy he was to, at last, have his own land.

There were dozens of young men getting homesteads, walking from God knows where, with no horses, or cows or anything — just them, putting in six months of each year for three years in order to "prove up." They would work on some farm near Moose Jaw in the summer and stay on their homesteads in the winter, and like as not sell out at the end of that time to some family man who was staying and making a home there.

One old fellow, by the name of Stewart, homesteaded right where the town of Briercrest stands now. He never did build a shack, just dug a hole in the side of a hill on the bank of the coulee and lived there. He was a queer old man and we were afraid of him. He used to dress in rags from his head to his feet; his legs were wound with torn gunny sacks and tied with string. He would walk from his place to Drinkwater for his groceries, a distance of about fifteen miles, and bring his food home on his back.

One day, Clyde and I saw him heading for Drinkwater, so we got on horseback and went to see his place out of sheer curiosity. It was unbelievable — the dirt, a pile of gunny sacks and an old horse blanket on the sod floor for his bed, a box for his table and a couple of stumps for chairs. It frightened me and I made Clyde shut the door quickly for fear some evil spirit would strike us dead.

There was the Glen family about five miles from us. They lived in a little valley and had been there for twelve years and had only forty acres plowed in all that time. We couldn't see their place from ours because of a hill. They went to the Coventry school north of them and never really belonged to the Briercrest district, until years after.

There was the Evans family from Wales — a lot of boys and one girl, Mary, who is nearly a hundred years old now and living in an old folks home in Moose Jaw. They had one of the first buggies in the country and Mr. Evans was so big he filled the seat of the buggy and kind of overflowed toward the dashboard as he drove to town.

The Elliot family came from Dakota — father, mother, a

grown-up girl and a boy of eleven. Mr. Elliot had a hard time gathering up four horses and a few implements to farm with. By the time he had paid for this poor second-hand stuff, he was broke. How to get his little family to Canada was beyond him. Only one person was allowed to ride free with settlers' effects cars. So he built a shelter in one end of the settlers car and piled hay over it. The night before they were to leave on the freight train, he waited until midnight when no one was around, herded his little family into the car, put them in the shelter he had fixed up, and when the train pulled out at dawn, no one knew that there were three extra passengers on it.

They were scared stiff at the border when the inspector came along to check on their car. But the father had warned them, on pain of death, that if anyone let out a squeak he would kill him. No one moved; everyone just held his breath until Mr. Elliot got the all-clear signal; the train started and they crossed the line and were safe. How they used to laugh about it, and tell how white old Bill (as he was called) was, until he got the "all clear" and saw the wheels starting to turn.

When they got their homestead, about three miles from us, they found to their dismay that there was no water on the Elliot farm — not even a slough that might tide them over for the summer. So poor old Bill had to draw water for his stock and the house from the creek near Drinkwater — about eight miles — in barrels in a lumber wagon.

He was a great man to "cuss"; the swear words just came tumbling out when he got mad, which was pretty often. When he got a few dollars saved he got in a well-digging machine and down they started. No dice. No water. Nothing. Just dry earth as far as the digger would go. So they would fill up the hole and when Bill got a few more dollars saved up, he'd get in the well diggers and try once more. He never did get water.

About thirty years after, some oil company came along and for a few dollars they bargained with the people who had bought his place to let them dig a well and hunt for oil. Square between the house and the barn they started to dig. I don't know how far they got down but they struck water, a great hidden reservoir of it that almost blew the auger out of the ground. It shot twenty-five feet in the air and then started to flow downhill — millions of gallons. It made a little creek and flowed for two miles downhill, making a small lake until the neighbors living there sent for a Mountie (the law of the country) and demanded that the well be filled in. It was and I would hate to think what Bill would have said if he was still alive.

Incidentally, they didn't strike oil either.

The lack of water was one of the curses of the country. We had a couple of big sloughs that saved us from drawing water for a time, but toward fall even they would go dry. My brother, Bruce, dug thirteen wells on his place across the road from us, but never did get what you might call a good well. That is the story of the whole settlement. Now and then a lucky man would strike a flow, but it was dry country and remains so to this day.

So they dug ponds. Nearly every farm had its pond and some of them are there yet, almost overgrown with little bushes and cattails and willows where birds nest and fill the sky with their songs.

When dad got a little money saved, he decided that he would take the gamble and sent for the well diggers. When they arrived with their high derrick and little engine to run the auger, we kids were wild with excitement. There were three men with the outfit — rough, dirty, hard-working men who knew their jobs and didn't lose any time; they just started the engine and down they went — twenty feet, forty, sixty, a hundred, but no water — nothing but sand and gravel and blue gumbo. Once they hit a layer of pure white sand; it was like talcum powder and dry as dust.

They gave up at 100 feet. Then they made a bargain with dad; they would try another hole at half-price. They got a tiny bit of water there, but not enough to water even a team of horses. Then they took another chance and moved about a quarter-of-a-mile east, down a little hill to what they called the flats. But it was the same old story — never enough to do. I can remember how oily the water in that low well was. It had to be baled out every other day or the horses wouldn't drink it.

Then dad dug a pond, scooping out the solid earth with shovels and pickaxes. But one day a neighbor came along and saw what he was doing and offered him the loan of a scraper that the horses could pull. He said, "You'll never dig a pond with a shovel. It would take you a hundred years." So dad hitched the quiet team to it and before long they had a fine pond, about 200 feet long, 50 wide and 12 feet deep. It was a godsend, for now we would have soft water for washing too. The wells were pure alkali and so hard that the soap would curdle when we tried to wash in it, and no amount of lye or water softener could make it soft.

CHAPTER 9

The First
Furrow

The four wild broncos dad had bought in Moose Jaw were wild beautiful horses that had never seen a wagon or plow in all their lives, and to get them hitched to a plow was a miracle, or a disaster, whichever way you like to put it.

Two of the horses were fairly easy to break; a nice brown one called Bess and a lovely white mare called Molly made a team. The other two, Minnie and Fly, were beautiful sorrel horses with slim legs, and wild as the winds of Montana. Fly was rightly named, for she would let fly her heels if anything living came near her. She could kick the very stars out of the sky.

She had a mean way of just quietly standing with her head down and then, bang, out would go her two hind legs with a wallop that could kill a man instantly. It was a miracle that she didn't kill anyone.

Getting them hitched was a daily miracle, too. Dad would make us three little girls get up on the roof of the barn for safety's sake. It was a low shanty-roofed barn, and he knew we were safe there. We wouldn't have missed the Wild West show that always went on when they were getting the horses hitched to the plow. I can remember yet the thrill of it — poor old Fly walking around the yard on her hind legs, Minnie stomping and squealing and often just lying down, the other two more quiet ones quivering and ready to bolt the first chance they got, and poor dad cussing and almost crying as he worked at getting them backed to the plow, hitched and started down to the place where he was working.

The first summer dad broke forty acres. Some of the furrows were crooked as a ram's horn — here and there a half-yard wide, some barely three inches. Sometimes the plow skimmed along on top of the "prairie wool", other places it gouged deep into the prairie soil cutting through brier roots that had woven a mat below the earth like a bird's nest, strong and tough, holding the soil together like a million tiny fingers.

But furrows they were — the first ones ever broken in the country that stretches from the Soo line south to the Dirt Hills and on to the American border eighty-four miles away.

It might not seem much, but it really was a miracle. Now great tractors turn over six to eight furrows at a time, but I doubt if the men, looking back at them, ever get the heart-warming satisfaction that dad got when he reached the end of the furrow, crooked and skimmed here and there, but brown and sending out a fragrance that has no name — dark, beautiful earth that had lain there since the beginning of time. And looking back across the years, I know now that it really looked like the crazy signature of a man's name, written upon the face of the prairie forever and ever.

My father rode the plow. (He had never ridden one before in his life.) Bruce ran on the plowed land, driving one team of horses. The plain fact is that he didn't drive at all. He just tried to keep abreast of the plow, with dad howling and yelling and waving a black snake whip in the wind that now and then caught around a kid's neck or legs with a sting that sent him or her howling home to be comforted by my mother, to be kissed and given a cookie to heal the wound.

Clyde, in his blue stocking cap, with another pair of lines running on the grass side of the plow, would also be trying to keep up. It's surprising they didn't drop dead from sheer exhaustion.

Behind the cavalcade, we three little girls would run panting and gasping for breath. If you have ever driven broncos, you'll know they never walk; they either run or refuse to move at all. When dad got them going he never dared stop for fear they'd lie down, poor beasts.

37

By the end of the day all were dead on their feet, the horses as well as the humans.

We didn't know then, that bright summer with meadow larks singing in the still blue air, that from those crooked furrows would go out a million fine straight ones; it would become acres and fields and townships and from that rich new earth millions of bushels of wheat would be grown; it would come to be known as one of the richest farming lands in the world.

What bounteous crops we had, forty to fifty-five bushels to the acre of number one — hard, plump and a deep natural color — the best wheat in the world for bread flour.

Oats often went a hundred bushels to the acre; my brother had a field of White Banner oats that went 115 bushels to the acre. The stooks were so close together you couldn't drive a hay rack between them.

Year after year the golden grain was threshed until the granaries were bursting full, and they left it in huge piles on the ground until they could draw it to the railroad ten miles away.

It almost seemed that Mother Nature, overjoyed to see the settlers coming in, put on her sweetest smile and fairest show to lure more and more to her prairies, pouring her riches out with a lavish hand like a good mother feeding a favorite child.

And now the scent of wild roses brings it all back to me, as if time itself turned back the pages and let us taste and feel and smell the fragrant earth black and good and warm from the sun.

Forty years later I was thinking of the early days and wrote this poem:

TO A HOMESTEADER

Pushing the frontiers further
    Back with relentless hands
Blazing a trail with a plowshare,
    Far in the hinterlands,
Holding fast to their birthright
    Born to the realm of toil,

Bearded grim and unconquered,
 Ragged kings of the soil.

Building their lonely cabins
 Staking their homestead claim,
Beating a trail to somewhere,
 Steady, fearless and fame,
Bounded by sky and muskeg,
 Hedged by the vast unknown,
Earning their hundred and sixty,
 Winning their fight alone.

Theirs is the dream eternal,
 Hills that are rugged and green,
Lure of the far horizons,
 Prairies wind-swept and clean,
Visioning towns in the making,
 Faith in the untried lands,
Holding the country's future,
 Safe in their calloused hands.

• • •

As I said before, dad always made us sit on the barn when he was getting the horses hitched together, and to this day I can feel the rutted edges of the shingles and smell their fragrance as the sun warmed the cedar up. From this high perch we learned many things that teachers never knew or had forgotten.

So the roof became a grandstand for us. Here with the coppery blue sky above we watched the drama of life before us in the wake of bucking broncos, runaway horses, wild cows being roped and milked, while dad and my two brothers (ages fourteen and seventeen) strutted their lines (not always fit for childish ears I am afraid), full of the good rigor of pioneer life. I assure you, none of the scenes were phony and there were no stand-ins for those pioneers who played their parts with bravery and often desperation and fear. But play them they did, and they opened up a new country for the new settlers. Most of them stayed and today their sons and grandsons farm the rich

39

land. Their names go on in little children and their blood flows warm and red in newborn babies with crumpled fists who some day will guide plows or ride combines or build ships.

Now and then you come across a bit of pasture whose native grass has never been broken up, and a nostalgia sweeps over your heart for the old days. You see (as if on a screen) that first furrow, crooked as a ram's horn, and smell the sweat of tired horses and hear the meadow lark's song; and you're young again, sitting on top of the barn and feeling strangely part of it all.

CHAPTER 10

Gentle Memories

I never remember our house when it wasn't full of company. I don't know how my mother stood it; I really think she enjoyed it as much as they did. She could whip up a meal in fifteen minutes that would stay with you for hours, warm and comforting like good wine after a long day's work.

There was no problem about food. We grew everything in the way of vegetables that you could think of; for meat, there were chickens running around the yard getting fatter every day, turkeys, ducks, pigs in their pens fat as seals, young steers in the pasture; with our own eggs, butter, cream and milk, for what more could you ask?

And mother loved to cook; she was never as happy as when she was cooking up a meal, watching us eat it, smacking our lips and praising her cooking.

In the year or so before the school started, I don't know how my father stood us. For no matter what he was doing around the farm, we were at his heels, watching, talking, helping (we thought). He wasn't that good-natured, nor were we overly fond of him; but I suppose he was where the action was. So we hung on his coat tails and knew everything that was going on.

If he were killing a pig, his favorite method was to get into the pen, where there would be three or four pigs fattening up. He'd select the one he wanted, lift and shove it over the top of the poplar-pole pen, pick up his gun, get the pig running and shoot it, then stick it wherever the poor thing happened to fall.

One day he got an especially lively one on the run, with us three kids chasing it and laughing and falling. He aimed at the pig a half-dozen times but didn't dare to shoot because one of us was too close. Finally he gave up in disgust and went into the house in a rage. My mother could hardly keep from laughing at the look on his face.

We found the pig about a week later at our nearest neighbor's, calmly eating some spilled oats; dad got him right there, shot him and dragged him home on the stone boat.

If dad went to the pond for water for the house, we were there at his heels. If he was pacing out a "land", we were following him. Even if he was just doing the chores, we were there. Yet, although he wasn't a good-natured man, I cannot remember him getting cross. Maybe he liked it.

In 1906 Bruce finished his homestead duties on the quarter just south of our homestead, and dad's brother, Uncle Johnny, came west from Colborne and bought it. There was no house on it; Bruce lived at home while putting in his "time", which was three years.

When Uncle Johnny and Aunt Phoebe came out, dad built a nice house for us with five bedrooms, a big living room, a kitchen and pantry. Uncle Johnny bought our little homestead house and they pulled it down to his quarter, a half-mile south, where it is to this day, standing forlorn and lonely and tilted to one side like a tired old man.

The years that followed were gentle and filled with peace. It would almost seem that the prairies had not yet learned the ornery ways of men. The summer days were golden-hued and filled with a kind of glowing light.

The nights were star-strewn, and somehow you got the impression of peaceful breathing, as if the land had only come awake with the arrival of man.

The flats to the east of us were filled with a radiant moonlight in which night birds sang and the little wild things came out to chase each other in joyful play along the padded trails that went from mound to mound. There were gophers, badgers, tiny red foxes, coyotes and now and then a shy deer flitting by in the white moonlight.

The sloughs were filled with clear blue water that reflected the sky and clouds, the sunset and the sunrise; they were homes for the wild fowl that came back to raise their broods and swim in the grass-scented water and eat from the wheat fields until they were so fat and heavy they could hardly fly when the time came for them to go south.

There were prairie chickens by the thousands. I remember my brother shooting them from the kitchen door. They were fat as butter and no better fowl ever flew than the brown prairie chicken of the early years.

Finally, there were mallards and canvas backs, pin tails and little gray snipe, and in the fall the great Canada Geese came down to feed in the grain fields, sometimes staying a week to fatten up for the rest of the journey south.

CHAPTER 11

Mr. Coventry's
Kindness

The day they branded the calves was always a red-letter day for us. Dad would rake all the old hay and straw from around the front of the barn right down to the earth. Then he'd build a little bonfire, carefully raking the soil up around it so the fire couldn't spread.

He'd lay the branding iron on the fire so it would get good and hot. While he was doing this, my sisters and I would climb the ladder and get on top of the haystack in order to get a better view of the show.

When the iron was almost red-hot, the calf would be brought out from the barn, its two front legs tied together and the two back ones; then the rest of the rope would be tied around its poor frightened body and it would be thrown to the ground, close to the fire and branding iron.

Clyde would sit on its head, Bruce on its rump, and dad would get the hot iron, poise it directly above the shoulder of the calf and come down hard, holding the handle of the iron in a death grip. As the hot metal ate into the hair and flesh of the animal, it would let out a terrified bawl of pain and terror. But dad would hang on with both hands until he was sure the brand had done its work, his face white; then he'd leap up, drop the iron and get out of the way as the boys unloosed the ropes and let the calf leap away, still bawling.

During all this, we three would be watching every move. The minute the calf started bawling we would start too, wailing like banshees, in sympathy, with dad shouting to us to, "Shut up."

To this day I cannot see why we went out to see the branding. Why didn't we just stay in the house, and not get our feelings harrowed up for the day; but we always went and to this day I can see the calf bounding away behind the barn, and the brothers going into the barn to get the next victim.

One morning our kindly friend, Francis Coventry, rode along on his lovely saddle horse. He wore a white cowboy hat and looked for all the world like President Teddy Roosevelt, my first hero.

That morning the horses were especially wild, kicking and standing on their hind legs as dad and the boys strove to get them harnessed and hooked together. All this went on in the yard; poor dad was white and Clyde was crying.

Mr. Coventry saw this as he rode into the yard. I can hear him yet, saying, "Tut . . . Tut . . . this will never do. You'll never get those two bay mares tamed. They're outlaws, pure and simple. I'll tell you what we'll do. I'll trade you a nice, quiet, well-broken team of horses for them and I'll put them out on the ranch in the hills. I just can't stand to see you killed or maimed before my eyes."

And so the deal was made. It was just a trade, and no deal before or since was such a lucky one for us. He brought the two old plugs over one morning, Kit and Farmer, and they saved not only lives but sanity. They proved quiet and steady. They knew more about plowing than dad ever did; they would keep in the right furrow, plugging along from one end of the half-mile; they knew when to turn at the end, sort of hauling the other two with them. And from then on, dad quieted down and the whole family heaved sighs of relief.

I might also add that dad had bought a wild unbroken pony for us kids. We never did get on his back. Bruce and Clyde got as far as jumping on him now and then, but they didn't last long. You'd see them flying through the air, arms and legs stretched out. Mr. Coventry saw this too, so he traded us a quiet old pony and took the wild one out to his ranch also. And old Dell became the very backbone of our lives, quiet and easy to ride, a real blessing if a horse is ever a blessing.

CHAPTER 12

The Picnic
to the Hills

The picnic to the hills was the highlight of the summer. We always held it on the first of July. It was the only outing of the year.

I couldn't sleep a wink the night before; I would just lie there in bed with my little sister, getting up a dozen times to look out the little narrow window and see if it was getting daylight, maybe drop off to sleep for a few minutes and then spring up again and see dawn coming up across the flats. And there is no more glorious sight on this earth than the sun slowly rising on the prairie, filling the summer world with colors that defy description. First a faint pink, then the full blooming of dawn — green, orange, yellow and always that sense of wonder at the vastness of the earth from rim to rim — empty and silent, yet filled with a strange breathing like wings above the house.

Meadow larks would be piping their songs, hundreds of them. The rooster would let out a few squawks; the dog would shake himself and wander towards the barn, as if to reassure himself that all was well; the hens would come out of the hen house door, ruffling their wings and start to hunt for food. The old cow on her tether would rise and stretch and start to eat as if to say, "Well, get up everyone. It's another day."

By this time we three girls would be dressed. There were no "outfits" for us, just nice little print dresses, the good ones we had been saving for the occasion.

We could hear dad in the kitchen making the fire, cussing a bit under his breath and yelling at maw to hurry.

Breakfast would be a hurried meal: good oatmeal porridge, big slices of homemade bread with syrup, and homemade butter. Dad and the boys would each eat a big slice of fried pork. Maw would have her tea; there was no tea for kids in those days, just milk or water gulped down in a hurry for fear we'd miss something.

Water would be left in pans in the yard for the chickens; the milk would be strained and set in blue pans in the cellar; the mother hens were left in their little overnight houses with slats for the little chickens to run in and out; the pigs were fed with extra rations; cows were freshly tethered on their long ropes and horses were fed.

My mother would have made most of the lunch the night before and packed in the blue bread pan: homemade head cheese, potato salad, radishes and little green onions, and maybe a bit of leftover Christmas cake, a raisin pie and her good homemade cookies.

Old Kit and Farmer would be hitched to the lumber wagon with dad and maw on the spring seat, we three in the back of the wagon as usual, laughing and wild with excitement. As the hills would loom nearer, we would see a few trees, our first glimpse of them since the picnic the year before.

The trail headed due south, winding here and there with a little curve around a gopher or badger hole, past Gallaugher's, Fraser's, Espelein's, where there was a tiny coulee to cross. Dad would ease the horses down the little bank and splash through the creek, maybe two feet of water in it, and then up the far bank, the horses flopping and scrambling for a foothold as if we were crossing the river Jordan.

Ahead, the hills would beckon, rising blue and lovely against the sky; the horses would trot along quietly as if they too were enjoying the break from the monotonous prairie and the plow.

My two brothers, Bruce and Clyde, would ride their horses; no wagon for them. Now and then they would pass us at a gallop, then circle back and race away again, leaving a little cloud of dust that settled down on the sage bushes and short grass, described by the oldtimers as "prairie wool".

Our destination would be "old Buchanan's ranch", exactly

twelve miles south of our homestead. He would come out to meet us with his dog, smiling and glad to see another human being, I suppose.

The ranch cattle and horses, hearing us come, would get on top of the hill behind the house and view us from afar, half afraid. There were trees there, real trees that we only saw once a year. My mother would almost cry and go over and pat them. And I know now how utterly homesick she must have been for the sight of a tree, and the smell of the leaves in her hand.

We kids would run up and down the little hills, tripping and falling and wild with joy just to be able to run up a hill. We'd take a drink of water from "Buchanan's spring" which was known all over the country as being the sweetest water on earth. How good it was, after the alkali water from our well or slough water with wigglers in it.

Dad would build a little fire to make tea, and we'd invite Mr. Buchanan to eat with us. They'd laugh and talk together.

For the first year or so there would be just us and two or three other families, but soon more settlers would join in and within five or six years there would be maybe fifty people out. Not many, I know, but fifty people in a new country was wonderful. The women would talk and laugh and compare notes on setting hens and new calves, and discuss how good it was to get out and talk to someone besides themselves.

Then it would be time to "hit for home" in the blue dusk of day, everyone quieter; we three kids in the back of the wagon were happy too, to be going home.

Toots, the dog, would come out to meet us, smiling, I swear, to see us back. The house and barn looked strangely comfortable in the quiet dusk — the cows waiting to be milked, the hens to be fed and their water pans filled up again. Then quietness would settle down and fold us in, as if the earth too was glad we were home safe and sound.

CHAPTER 13

The First
Church

Grandpa and Grandma Jaques were dyed-in-the-wool Methodists, real oldtimers who believed in hell-fire and the wiles of the Devil and all his tribe. They went sedately to church every Sunday morning, with their bit of collection tied in the corner of grandma's handkerchief, for fear grandad might lose it. They never swore, or told a lie, or did a dishonest thing in all their sober lives, as far as I know. They were Christians, simple and honest and with a fear of hell-fire in their hearts.

So, when we got settled in our first prairie house and a few neighbors came in, dad said we had better get a church started one way or the other. He started to hunt for a minister or missionary and found one in Rouleau, twelve miles east of us, by the name of Mr. Bard. I don't know what his first name was, but dad badgered him, and likely the church board in Rouleau, to have him come out and hold a little meeting in our house, for a start.

Then dad went around the little new settlement on horseback to tell the people about it. And so the minister came, driving a wild-eyed bronco hitched to a buggy across the trackless prairie with no road or landmarks of any kind, just a faint trail across the flats. The poor young fellow and the empty world he had come to, how frightened he must have been.

But he came. My mother would put down a couple of homemade mats on the floor that she carefully kept in a trunk under the stairs; she arranged a nice clean cloth on the top of the sewing machine, which he used for a pulpit. As I remember back, there was a sense of love and good will among us that was to last as long as they lived.

We three little girls sat on the bottom step of the stairs — no chairs for us. I remember Mr. Gallaugher (the first homesteader after us). I can see him sitting in dad's armchair in front of the stove, holding his little boy on his lap and trying to make him sit still while the sermon was on.

After about two years of this they got a little school started and services were held there. Everyone came: Methodists, Presbyterians, Catholics, Anglicans — all so glad to be able to get out and talk to someone, just anyone who would listen; they would show off their babies, patting the little ones on the head, exchanging bits of news from home — just glad to meet and laugh; then, people would go home in their wagons.

We used to go in our lumber wagon too, until my grandparents came out. After that we had to use a stone boat because grandma was fat and couldn't climb into the wagon fast enough for the broncos. We'd put a chair in the yard for her, but by the time she had huffed and puffed and got on the chair the broncos would be a quarter-of-a-mile away, and she'd be on the chair fanning herself with a little folding fan she had brought from Ontario. So we put the spring seat from the wagon on the stone boat and grandma rode like the queen of Sheba with a couple of kids holding the seat.

Grandpa homesteaded at the age of seventy-six. He didn't quite last out the three years, but the land office at Moose Jaw gave dad the title to the homestead anyway and grandma went back to Ontario.

They had a little shack on their quarter section of land, about twelve-by-twelve, and a much smaller house not far away. I can see my grandmother heading for the smaller house muttering to herself, wishing she were home in Collingwood where it was in the woodshed.

And so for nearly ten years the school was used for church and Sunday school. Box socials were held with a dollar limit. As dad would be the auctioneer, he never let them go beyond that; he knew they couldn't afford more, no matter how much they wanted a special girl. I remember old Mac McNaughton got my box once and he was so mad he never spoke to me all the while we ate. He thought he was getting Lizzie Findlay.

• • •

Around 1911, after the railroad came, dad got on the horse again and rode around the district and around the new little town, telling everyone that we had to have a real church, and we'd call it a "union" church so everyone would come.

But the split had happened. The Presbyterians built a church themselves. There was quite a bit of ill feeling and dissension. I remember going to their church one Sunday afternoon and sitting with old Mrs. Findlay and she said sadly to me, "I wish we were all back together, Edna, in the Sunnyhill school; we were better friends then."

In 1925 the real church union took place. It was a good thing; now we all knew where we stood, one way or the other. I was there in the lovely new church at Briercrest the Sunday it was made legal and we were glad. There was a fine service.

Nice harvest suppers have been served there, friends made and strangers welcomed. Perhaps we'll all be one in heaven; I hope so. As this is written in 1975 it is the golden anniversary of the United Church, as they call it now. It marks fifty years of trying and working, with harvest suppers and ladies aid, weddings, christenings (there were twenty-five children and babies christened that first Sunday), burials, young peoples' meetings and Sunday school.

Fifty years, and yet my heart remembers the first church held in the country and in our homestead house, using the top of the sewing machine for a pulpit.

CHAPTER 14

The
School

At first, there was no school within fifteen miles of us. So dad thought that with four school-age kids running wild on the prairie, we must have a school. He drove to Moose Jaw and got in touch with the right people. I don't know how he did it, but one day we saw a wagon load of lumber arrive in the yard with four men riding on it. They were the carpenters who had come to build a school. Dad took them to the place where the school was to be built, about a mile from our place.

I do not remember who donated the little half-acre for the school and yard, but next day dad paced off the land (he was great at pacing land) and the foundations of the school were set down. I think the school was about twenty-by-forty — big enough to seat twenty kids. There were three windows on each side, a little platform at one end, a huge coal-burning stove at the back, and ten seats, two kids to a seat.

The first day there was great excitement for everyone. Just thirteen kids showed up: among them were our four (Clyde, Edna, Madge, Arlie); Wyatts, two girls and a little boy; Mary and Bob Banks and their cousin, Lou Jacobs; Fred Elliot, and I don't remember the names of the rest. We were a shy bunch of kids, playing on top of a little pile of lumber, stealing glances at each other — suddenly shy at meeting for the first time.

We all walked to school, of course, carrying our lunches in shiny new lard pails; lunches usually consisted of a couple of slices of good homemade bread, hard boiled eggs, and if we were lucky, a couple of cookies.

The Wyatt kids had to walk over three miles each way. Poor little Homer was just six, and his fat little legs were so tired that the minute he got into school he would go to sleep; the kindly teacher would just let him sleep, in the morning anyway.

The teacher was Miss Russel from Ottawa — a quiet religious girl who read a chapter from the Bible before she gave us lessons; she seemed bewildered at the job she had got herself into. She didn't stay long. She was too gentle and shy for the new country and hated the hardship and cold and walking a mile to school at twenty below zero.

The first death was a baby — a little newborn. Its parents were Mr. and Mrs. Walter Hillson. Mrs. Hillson had been one of our early teachers and married the son of the people who owned the house where she was boarding. I don't know what happened. I was too young and careless even to feel badly about it, but I remember my mother crying over the little white body as she dressed it for its tiny burial.

My father and a couple of the neighbors drove to Rouleau twelve miles away to bury it, and my mother said, "It's the first death, but it won't be the last. We'll have to get a good graveyard started, nice and high so we can dig deep enough that the coyotes won't be able to get down to them."

Other teachers followed her, at about one per year. With the country filled with bachelor homesteaders, a new teacher was the talk of the country. "Did you see her? What does she look like? . . . Is she fat? . . . How tall is she?" But it wouldn't be long until they saw her for themselves. Some of them would call at the school with the pretext of looking for a lost horse, and ask her if she had seen it.

But she knew their tricks. Sometimes she would invite them in, put a chair for them on the platform, and go on with her work. Young fellows who never darkened the door of a church would come all spruced up, faces shining, hair slicked down, just go get a better look at the new teacher.

Teachers did well if they lasted a year. Half the country was filled with teachers. Girls from Ontario, New Brunswick,

P.E.I., hunting for experience sure got it: forty below zero for weeks on end, blizzards that shut them in for days at a time, loneliness that almost drove them mad, and sometimes, after they were married, they had their babies without doctors or even neighbor women to help them.

I remember one whose baby started to come a cold winter day. Her husband started for Rouleau, fifteen miles away, to get a doctor; he had a team and a sleigh, but when he got halfway there a raging blizzard started up and poor Tom got lost and landed on a farm about fifteen miles from where he was headed.

For hours the mother cried and yelled as the pains became unbearable. They had a hired man, a young fellow from Scotland, shy as only a young Scotsman can be. He stood it as long as he could. Then washing his hands, and putting on a clean shirt, he went to her and said, "Look, Misses, I can't stand any more of your screaming. I am used to helping the mother lambs in Scotland when they're in trouble, so I'll help you." After the baby was born, he made the mother comfortable, washed and dressed the baby, and laid it beside her, wrapped in a little white shawl.

When the blizzard died down, Tom came home almost afraid to come into the house. But there she was, sitting up in bed, everything cleaned up, having a cup of tea with her baby beside her. Poor Tom was so relieved, he kissed the hired man (before he kissed his wife or baby), and when the man was ready to go to his own homestead, Tom gave him a fine team of horses and helped him in a dozen different ways and was his friend as long as they lived.

CHAPTER 15

The Post Office

When my father decided we had better get a post office started, he drove to Rouleau and talked to the postmaster there, a Mr. Johnston; before we knew it, there was a little post office in their bedroom and they named it Briercrest (after the name of the homestead).

There were eleven families getting mail there and we got it twice a week from Rouleau. The mail was kept in their six-by-eight bedroom, in little pigeon holes nailed to the wall. Dad doled the mail out as if he owned every letter and newspaper and was only handing it out because he liked the people getting it.

How welcome the letters were to the homesick pioneers; there were letters from Ontario, queer little blue envelopes from England, creased and sometimes dirty but welcome as the flowers of May. The men would sit there in the kitchen, sometimes with tears running down their cheeks, sniffing and wiping their eyes with calloused hands, telling us about their mothers and families, kind of ashamed of their emotion; we could see them stopping in the yard and reading them over as if to memorize every word.

Later on dad built a little country store beside the house. The post office was partitioned off at one end and operated for almost ten years. We got to know everyone's family — where they lived and how they were getting along without their boys. But the Old Country and even Ontario were far away and I know some of them never saw their parents again.

Sometimes a letter would come from some far-away place, inquiring about a son whose last post office address had been Briercrest. They were pitiful letters, often from anxious parents who hadn't heard from them for a year or so and were worried sick.

Dad always tried to find out where the missing person was. Maybe he was someone's hired man or a well digger or just a drifter who left for parts unknown. Dad would drive or ride to the last place he had been seen and inquire about him; more often than not he would find him hale and hearty. Then he would bring out a small writing tablet and pencil and make him write a letter. He'd bring it home, put a stamp on it, and send it on; I know he eased many parents' hearts just by doing this little chore. Then, more often than not, he would get a letter of thanks.

He found one "missing person" a few miles away. Another he found in the hills, happily herding cattle. Once he traced a man who had been killed in a well. They didn't even know his last name, but the boss bought a coffin, dad read the burial service, and they put a little stone over the grave with only one word on it: "Jim". But, putting two and two together, they knew they had found the right boy. Someone with a tiny camera took a picture of the grave and the name on it, and sent it to his mother in Ontario.

One day an official letter came from one of the "big houses" in England, inquiring about a son. Dad hunted him down and found him riding a plow out near the hills; he told him about the letter and told him to write home. But the man became afraid and headed for South America. The next time I saw him was in London, where I had gone for the coronation. There he stood in his scarlet and gold uniform, in the third line behind the queen and looking just about the same as when he was pitching hay or riding a bronco, only a bit fatter.

CHAPTER 16

The Piano

Somewhere among my remote ancestors there must have been a musician, and maybe from his blood or heart the love of music and the making of it was passed on to me; but until I was nearly sixteen I didn't know I had the gift.

I had taken about twenty lessons in Collingwood from a quiet lady who lived near the Methodist church. I used to practice, observed by my mother who had her "spanker" within reach; a gentle tap of it would make me sit at the piano, trying to find the proper notes on the piano. I might say, I never got far.

Then one day on the homestead, I suddenly wanted to play music. All the tunes I knew from the Sunday school came flooding into my mind including, "Jesus Loves Me This I Know" and "God Sees the Little Sparrow Fall"; but what could I do without anything to play them on?

So I sent to Eaton's for a beginner's book, then found a clean board behind the barn, and with some black paint from dad's workshop I painted a keyboard on it. From this I learned a few songs, and then came a miracle.

One day, across the flats where there was no road, came a queer covered wagon, swaying from side to side. It disappeared below the hill, then came up over it like Noah's Ark, headed straight for our house. When it stopped a man's head stuck out from the driver's seat and he shouted, "Anybody home?" So we all rushed out and what did we see but a real piano; the queer part of it was that dad knew the man. He was from Collingwood

— Archie Lamont. So dad invited him in for dinner, and miracle of miracles, before Archie left, the piano was sitting in maw's bedroom and I was on the stool. I ran my fingers up and down the white keys and played without a stop, "God Save the Queen," and "When Johnny Comes Marching Home."

When I finished, dad turned to go out into the living room and there were tears running down his cheeks and I heard him mutter, "I don't know where she gets it, I just don't know." He went out shaking his head, filled his pipe, and sat looking out the window.

After that, whenever I heard someone playing I would rush over and sort of tape the tune in my head; when I got home I could play it. I am sure I know 200 tunes right now that I could play at a moment's notice. I might say that there was only one other piano in the country; it belonged to a Mrs. Mellor. They had come up from California to homestead, of all things. They finished their three years and proved up on the homestead and left the country, and we never heard of them again. My mother used to say there was something queer about them, for they were real city folk, well-dressed, beautiful manners and sure didn't look like homesteaders.

Of course there were no radios or televisions or phonographs in those days. We just picked the songs up at dances and Christmas concerts in the school; anywhere I heard anyone playing I was all ears and itchy fingers.

CHAPTER 17

Clyde's
Discovery

Again our kindly friend and neighbor, Mr. Coventry (if you can call anyone living twelve miles away, a neighbor), extended a helping hand to us. He offered dad six cows with their calves on "shares". That is, we were to keep them for three years and then give him back the original cows and their grown-up calves. We were to keep the extra calves that had been born; they were to be the beginning of a herd for us and as there was unlimited pasture for them, it was no problem. However, as it turned out there was a problem: water, or the lack of it.

That year was especially dry. All the sloughs dried up so I was elected to stay home from school (it ran in the summer too) and drive the cows to the coulee about five miles away, keep them there until late afternoon, let them drink all they wanted and then bring them home and into the corral to be milked at nightfall.

I had a good horse and a wonderful dog, a Border Collie from Scotland that one of the hill ranchers, Mr. Buchanan, had given us. Her name was Toots and she was so intelligent that dad declared she could talk; I wouldn't have been surprised if she had. I would go to the school in the morning, get the lessons of the day, then gather up my little herd and head for the coulee around noon with the cows.

They knew the way as well as I did, so I just kind of followed them. After we got there and the cows had a good drink, they would quietly start to eat and I would get out my reader and scribbler and do my lessons. Needless to say, I learned many of the poems and stories by heart. I believe I could quote most of my reader to this day: "Grey's Elegy," "Ode to a Skylark," "Death of a Tree," "The Vision of Mirza," "Edinburgh After Flodden," "The Black Prince." I also believe that either my horse or dog, if given speech, could have recited them from memory, word perfect, with sound effects.

Three summers of this did something to me. I don't know what you would call it, but it gave me a strong abiding peace that nothing has ever been able to take away. For, in the turbulent years that followed, when things reached a low ebb, I would go back into my memory of those prairie twilights, and envision the long line of cattle headed home (they wore a path three inches deep in the clean sod). And there would be that turquoise sky with a few stars just coming out, the vast plains remote and lonely, just me and the dog and horse, and the old corral of poplar poles at the end of the trail.

Likely as not, my father and mother would be waiting in the still dusk, their milk pails on their arms; there would be a little smudge fire burning — smelling of sage and tumbleweed and barnyard manure — to make a smoke.

By the time I was fourteen I was writing something every day, and keeping it carefully out of sight for fear of ridicule. But one day the blow fell. Clyde found me writing and wanted to know what I was doing. I tried to hide the paper but with very bad manners and a sweep of his long arm, he reached around and grabbed the paper and ran. He being older, and with much longer legs, it was hopeless from the start; so I stopped chasing him and he read it.

I'll never forget his face as he turned to me. It was lighted up and he said, "You didn't write this yourself. You couldn't." By this time I had a lump in my throat the size of your fist and could only nod, "Yes."

"Why," he said. "It's lovely, just lovely," and handed it back to me, asking if I had any more. I nodded again and he walked away toward the barn; I went into the house and put the poems back in their hiding place, between the rafters and a little cleat I had nailed to the wall in the far corner of the attic.

CHAPTER 18

My First
Editor

A little while after that, it was my turn to go to town, which was Moose Jaw about twenty-five miles away. Each one of us three little girls had one trip a summer. Clyde said to me, "Write out a few of your poems and I'll take them to the *Times*." So I wrote a few, rolled them up and tied them with a blue hair-ribbon and away we went.

We started out at dawn; the smell of sage was in the air and meadow larks were singing from every brier patch. The sky was red from rim to rim, and the horses jogged along as we sat happily swaying in the spring seat of the wagon, laughing and talking all the way. When we were about halfway to town we reached the creek, Clyde unhitched the horses, watered and fed them and we sat, propped up against the wheel of the wagon, eating our good hard boiled eggs and sweet cakes. We filled the lard pail at the creek and drank hungrily from the swift-flowing water, with never a thought of germs or wrigglers or anything else that might harm our innards.

In Moose Jaw we stayed at my cousin's overnight and early next day went down to the *Times,* Clyde carefully carrying the little rolled-up parcel, tied with a blue ribbon. "Now, don't be so frightened. I'll take them in and you won't have to say a word, just stand there and nod."

Then he said, "Here, you hold them while I dust off my pants." And, innocent as you please, I took them. Without a word, he opened the door, pushed me in, and stood on the outside holding the knob.

Through a blue haze I saw a kindly-faced man behind a huge desk, who I learned later was Thomas Miller, owner and editor of the *Times;* he was to become the lieutenant-governor of Saskatchewan. He never knew how big and imposing he looked to a scared little girl who was frantically trying to open the door and get out.

He smiled and said, "Have you something there for me?" I noded and he motioned for me to let him have it. I tiptoed gingerly across the red carpet and handed my poems fearfully to him, and backed up against the door. I watched him, my heart beating as if it would burst. He saw how frightened I was and he came around and placed a chair where I could look out the window, then started to hand me books that he took down from a row of shelves. Then he asked me a lot of questions, to all of which I merely nodded, yes or no. I was beyond speech of any kind.

Finally, he patted my shoulder and said, "You read these my dear, and when they are finished, come back for more, will you?" I nodded yes, but it was three good years before I summoned enough courage to go back.

I might say, he published the three poems and told me, years after, that quite a few people asked him who this Edna Jaques was, and when he told them I was a little girl who lived on a farm twenty-five miles away, they wouldn't believe him.

I later heard another version of the first visit, from Fred Workman, editor of the *Times Herald.* "After you went out," he said, "Mr. Miller came out to the composing room and said to the boys there, 'You see that little girl going up the street with her brother? Well, some day she'll write her name across Canada.'" And I think, with God's help, perhaps I have. Here is one of the poems:

> Just a long wide stretch of prairie
> Sullen as the wind goes by,
> Just a radiant bow of promise
> Flung against a stormy sky.
> Just a long low cry at midnight
> As a coyote calls its mate,

In the spirit of the frontier,
    Half of love and half of hate.

Just a high arched dome of splendor
    Somber since the moon had gone,
Just a bird's clear call of morning,
    Singing to the coming dawn,
Just an aching throbbing stillness
    And a solitude that pains,
The place God made and then forgot —
    The lonely trackless plains.

• • •

At sixteen I figured I'd had enough school and decided to quit. I had managed to pass the grade eight exam that came from Regina, and figured I had enough education to count all the cows I'd ever have, for at that time I wanted to be a rancher and live in the hills. So I brought my books home, and the next morning after breakfast, when dad stuck his head in the back door and bawled for someone to come out and turn the grindstone, I followed him out into the yard and began to turn it. After a few minutes he looked up and said, "Why aren't you at school?" I said, "I've quit," and that was that. I never went back and no one said a word to me about it.

But every time my mother went to town she brought home a load of books. I don't think her choice was especially good, but we devoured them like a pack of hungry wolves, and when we had gone through the lot, we read them again. My sister, Madge, who had a brilliant mind (she died years ago) used to pick books out of Eaton's catalogue for us and even today I marvel at her choice. We knew the *Rubáiyát of Omar Khayyám* forward and backward. We read English history, wept over *Oliver Twist* and Little Dorrit and Little Nell and her grandfather. In fact, for a long time I thought we were related to Little Nell, so vividly did my sister bring her before our eyes. I can see the picture of her yet, walking down the road with her round sailor hat, print dress and black-stockinged legs, holding to her grandfather's hand while the other one held a red bandana handkerchief and all her worldy goods.

I might mention here, that we are descended in some way from the Brontë sisters. One of them married a Linton; my grandmother Jaques was a Linton from Yorkshire and my sister Madge's second name was Linton. So maybe some of their genius, just a tiny bit of it, was passed down to us. For everyone in my family could have been writers; I was the only one who stayed with it.

I am sure we didn't get any writing talent from my father, for as far as I knew, he only read one book in his life, *The Brazen Hussy* by Bertha M. Clay. But he loved the almanac and when things got extra dull in the winter, he would read it from cover to cover. By the time he had finished it, he had every disease known to man or woman. Then he'd go into the pantry and take a dose of every kind of medicine there, a couple of Lydia Pinkham's Pink Pills — they were for women but he took them anyway — a dose of nitre, a pinch of saltpeter, a headache pill the size of a quarter, and likely as not, a dose of salts, which is probably the only thing that saved his life.

CHAPTER 19

Prairie
Fire

The Soo Line from Moose Jaw to Portal was about ten miles north of us, but there were no villages or towns nearby. There was a place called Drinkwater, where there was a huge water tank with water pumped up to it from the creek or river for the C.P.R. trains, but there were no buildings. Then one day a man by the name of Andy Sipes came along and put up a tiny grocery store, just a shack really, and from then on we could get our groceries there.

One day, in the fall of the year, Bruce was sent to town for groceries and it was my turn to go, as we three little girls had to take turns going places; I suppose they couldn't stand the three of us at one time.

There was no bridge, but we crossed the river by walking a narrow plank about twelve inches wide, on top of the dam. If we fell on one side we would drown, and if we fell on the other side we would dash our heads against rocks. But we managed to creep over and then walk up to the store about a mile away.

We got our groceries, and one item on the list was a 100 pound bag of flour. Poor Bruce got it loaded onto his shoulder, somehow, and started back to the wagon on the other side of the dam. Then his poor tired legs just buckled up under him, and down he went, the flour on top of him. He just lay there like a dead man for about fifteen minutes until he got his wind. I don't know how he got that hundred weight of flour up again on his shoulder, for he wasn't a big boy; but he got it there, and managed to walk the slippery twelve-inch plank across the dam, to the team and wagon.

I struggled after him, pretty tired too, but glad to be past the worst of it, I thought.

As we rested there, Mr. Gutteridge, who ran the pump for the C.P.R. tank, came down to speak to us. He said, "You can't hit out tonight for your place. There is a terrible prairie fire coming in from the hills; you'd be burnt to death. So unhitch the horses and we'll get barrels of water on the stone boat, and wet bags, and if it gets this far, we'll be ready for it."

So they all went out fighting the fire. I was given a blanket and told to go to sleep on the floor, which I did; I slept like a log, ate a good breakfast and Mr. Gutteridge said he thought it would be safe to start out as the smoke was clearing and the fire seemed to have burnt itself out.

After we got about five miles from their place, we struck the burnt prairie, black as your hat. I don't know what stopped the fire, for as far as you could see there was just the crunchy black earth; here and there a piece of tumbleweed or sagebrush was smoking.

Bruce was worrying for fear our folks had been burnt out, but when we rounded the tiny hill before our place, we could see the little house standing, alone but triumphant, like a lone sailor who had managed to survive a wreck. I might say here, that now, after seventy years, that same homestead house still stands, leaning a bit like an old man.

We always had a wide fireguard (a strip of plowed land) around our farm buildings. It was the boundary that my mother set for us. We were never to go farther from the house than the fireguard, and to this day I find myself using the old term. Only recently I warned my little grandson not to go "past the fireguard," and then had to laugh at myself for using the old term.

CHAPTER 20

The
Bridge

My dad didn't appear to be extra smart, but he'd sit in his old red armchair and look out the window to the west, and the next thing you knew, he was starting something new.

We needed a bridge over the river near Drinkwater. Up to that time we had to row across or walk the dam, as I said before, and then walk the mile to the little village. As that was the nearest store (this side of Moose Jaw, twenty-five miles away), there just had to be a bridge.

So, one day dad started planning it and I don't know to this day who he badgered in Moose Jaw, but before we knew it there was a fine bridge and everyone rejoiced. It still stands, sort of bent in the middle, but it is there, looking rather smug in its old age, carrying its seventy years as if it were to hang on forever.

Getting telephone service was the same; that far back a telephone was a novelty. Only the rich people who lived in town had them and there were no phones in the homesteaders' shacks, I can tell you. I don't know who he badgered this time, but they told him he had to have eleven subscribers or no phones. Well, he got ten all right, more out of the novelty of the thing than anything else.

But the eleventh was different. They were Germans by the name of Banks, who had come from Regina. Mrs. Banks was afraid of phones, she thought they might blow up any time and set the house on fire. Dad went to her coaxing, begging, threatening to run her out of the country if she didn't take the phone (it seems she was the boss in the family). Dad finally wore her down and she consented to have it; but she insisted that it be put on the porch; she wouldn't have it in the house.

But she was still afraid of it and for the next week she slept in the barn, until one night there was a terrible electric storm. As she was afraid of that too, she came back into the house. She said she didn't sleep for a week, but the family laughed her into a good humor. But she never spoke a word over it, as long as they stayed there.

Dad also became a justice of the peace and signed papers for half the country. He dealt with sale of land, proof of homesteads and Americans coming in to buy land or getting their citizen's papers. He was also involved with the selling and buying of the homesteads the young fellows had 'proved up' on; many left for the cities as they found it too lonely living by themselves. Dad must have done all right, as there wasn't any backfire that I can remember.

When old Mrs. Lynds died, he not only took the body to Rouleau to be shipped back to Salt Lake City, he made all the difficult arrangements necessary to have a dead body shipped across the border into the U.S.A.

He was a sort of father confessor for the whole community too. If a husband and wife had a fight, the man often would come to dad and ask him what he should do. We would give him a good meal and let him talk himself out, and toward sunset he would give a sheepish grin and say, "Well, I guess I'd better give it another try. After all, my wife is a good woman and works hard. I don't know what I'd do without her." Dad would make one of us drive the man home and leave him at his own door; as far as I know, the cure always worked.

Sometimes, if a father or mother got sick and had to drive to Rouleau to the nearest doctor, they would bring the kids to our place, unload them at the kitchen door with a few instructions as to what to do with them, and drive on, quite confident that the kids would be all right until they came back for them, whether it was a few days or two weeks, depending on the sickness. I never remember when we didn't have from one to five extra kids in the house. Now, years later, I marvel at my mother who never seemed to mind either their presence or the food they would eat, or any other discomfort they caused. When their parents came back, they just drove up to the door, got their kids, and took them home; I know there was never any question of payment. Maybe my father and mother will be paid in better coin in heaven.

CHAPTER 21

Celebrations

My mother had a joyfulness of spirit that I have often envied. She loved the special days of the year and always devised something to set them apart.

She'd started on New Year's Eve when we still lived in Collingwood. We three little ones would be sound asleep in our beds upstairs, but when the bells of the old Methodist church would start to toll the old year out, up she would come and wake us. I still remember the bells; I would shiver; they sounded as if they were tolling a death.

She had a picture that she brought up to show us, of a bent old man, "Father Time" she called him. He had long white matted hair, wore a ragged shirt and was old and tired and ugly. I used to feel sorry for him as he toiled up toward the Pearly Gates, knowing his work on earth was done, and going back into heaven.

Then after a few minutes of the sad music and the bells, she would bring out another picture of the "Little Boy New Year," and he would be coming out of the clouds to take Father Time's place.

The little boy had curly golden hair, a pair of tiny wings and little fat feet. He would be smiling and the bells would have a joyful sound like a schottische or a Highland fling; she would show us his picture and pat us and tell us he was the Little Boy New Year; then she would go downstairs and we'd go back to sleep, safe and warm in our beds.

The next celebration was my birthday, January 17; there

was always a little gift and a cake. Next was my sister Madge's birthday on January 30, and again the gift and a cake. Then my youngest sister, Arlie, had her birthday on February 6. After that, February was kind of dull; they didn't go in for Valentines, that I remember.

Then St. Patrick's Day would arrive March 17 and all the stops were out for him. Green tissue paper streamers were strung from the hanging lamp above the table to everyone's plate, there were bunches of artificial shamrocks (where she got them I'll never know, but they were there), a lovely cake with green icing, and a special roast of beef: even the sides of that had green tissue paper wrapped around it. Dad would snort, but I think he enjoyed the special supper, even though he wouldn't admit it.

In Collingwood, April slipped by. But May 24 loomed up before us — the queen's birthday. School was closed; there would be a parade with kids dressed in white dresses carrying the Canadian flag. In one corner there was a small flag of England on a red background, and in the lower corner, the coat of arms of the Dominion. How we loved it and revered the good Queen Victoria, whose reign saw England rise from a rather small country into an empire whose possessions circled the world, and on which the sun never set.

Summer holidays passed, two long beautiful months of play and fun with picnics and little trips here and there, and maybe an excursion on dad's boat to Christian Island.

After we moved to Saskatchewan, mother kept up the celebrations. Some cousins came west too, and went into business in Moose Jaw. They would always come out for Christmas. They would get up around five in the morning, have breakfast and start out to our place (twenty-five miles in the dead of winter), with a team of horses and a sleigh, blankets, hot bricks in the straw, and warm overcoats.

Sometimes the snow would be so deep the poor horses could hardly pull the sleigh. It would take a good three hours to make the trip, but they would arrive, jolly and full of laughter at seeing us. My mother would have a feast ready: the biggest turkey in the yard, prime dressing, pickles, cranberry sauce, great pots of potatoes, turnips, carrots, her delicious Christmas

71

cake and plum pudding; I don't know who enjoyed it more, her, or the visitors who groaned and declared they couldn't eat another bite but kept on eating.

Then, after celebrating the birthday of the Prince of Peace, our cousins would make the long drive home in the moonlight over the white prairie; there would be hardly a sleigh mark to show them the way, only the still empty world.

Long years after, I wrote this poem:

THE MOTHER AT CHRISTMAS

Thy birthday Lord . . . the prickly holly tree,
Bears its red bitter fruit to honor Thee.

The cedar boughs that twine about the stores,
The scarlet wreath beside the open doors.

A lighted candle shining warm and bright,
Shepherds abiding in the fields by night.

Gray huddled sheep . . . and suddenly a star,
Shining upon the hilltop where they are.

The song of angels . . . suddenly to them,
The lighted road that leads to Bethlehem.

And for the world forever God's new grace,
Reflected from a child's wee shining face.

CHAPTER 22

Buckwheat
Pancakes

I wonder if people still eat buckwheat pancakes, the old-fashioned kind that you start in the fall in a heavy crock and keep going all winter. Do they still make them in country kitchens, the air blue with smoke and grease, and little blobs of slopped-over batter burning on the stove?

My mother used to start them, not too early in the fall, just when the mornings began to get real cold. We'd be getting along fine on fried potatoes and pork or porridge, toast and syrup, and then one day dad would begin, "Say, when are we going to start the buckwheat pancakes?" and suddenly everyone in the house would get hungry for them as if they had been hungry all the time and didn't know what ailed them.

Maw would hum a little tune (she always started new things by singing a tune.) She would dig up the old heavy brown pitcher she made them in, and begin to stir up a batter: first a pinch of salt, then two cups of warm water and a yeast cake, two tablespoons of brown sugar (to help the yeast grow), a few handfuls of white flour, and four handfuls of buckwheat flour. That's the way she measured verything, by the handful, and the pancakes were started on their way.

She'd let them rise in a cool place — usually the window sill of the pantry — until the next night, when the mixture would be bubbling and alive. Then she'd add a few more cups of warm water (depending on the crowd she had to feed), a few more handfuls of white flour, and then enough course brown buckwheat flour to make a good batter that would pour easily.

This was set in the pantry for the night, and by morning it was always running over the top and ready for the baking.

We had an old-fashioned griddle, half the size of the cookstove; this was allowed to get smoking hot and dad would stand with a thick slice of salt pork on a fork and grease the griddle; then the batter was poured on in little precise rounds that baked quickly. A quick flip with the turner and the other side was browned to perfection, carried to your plate and flopped down with a satisfied grunt from dad; I have yet to taste anything on earth that can beat buckwheat pancakes on a cold winter morning.

Of course you had to have a good slice of fried salt pork to go with them, and syrup to sweeten the whole plateful. But you had something, a warm filling meal that stayed with you for hours, whether you drove a load of wheat to town at forty below or went to the hills and cut wood, or just did chores.

Now when I see city people sitting down to a breakfast of a cup of coffee and a cigarette, I am sorry for them; they don't know what they're missing.

When life crowds in on me and I am tired and worn and busy, I sit and think about the old breakfasts we used to have at home; I am heartened and comforted by the remembrance of a pile of buckwheat pancakes, swimming in syrup with a good slice of salt pork on the side of the plate waiting for me.

CHAPTER 23

Seed
Potatoes

There is something about a potato with a sprout on it that rings a bell in my heart. I opened a new bag of potatoes recently and brought a dozen or so of them up for dinner; I hated to cook them, for every one had the grandest sturdy sprout, about an inch long, coming out of the top of it (the seed end), sort of furry, a pale new lavender color and as full of life as an acorn. Strong new life coming up from the heart of the old one, bursting through the rough brown jacket, clamoring for light, its little seeking lips calling out for sod and rain and warm sweet air.

We know winter is really over when the potatoes begin to sprout in the cellar. We know the little pulse inside of them has begun to beat, urging them to wake up and get ready to do their work in the world. The little sunken dead eyes begin to open (like kittens in the dark), and there is movement and life within the wrinkled brown coat; the tide is coming in so strong and vital that the smallest living thing responds to it and is lifted up.

My mother used to love to cut seed potatoes. She loved the rough feel of them in her hand. She'd turn one over and over, caressingly, taking her time to see just where would be best to cut it; she'd cut through the seed end first, halving that, explaining to us that if it was allowed to grow in one piece the potatoes would all be little ones and crowded, like too many birds in a nest, and that would never do.

She'd sit on an upturned box or keg at the end of the garden, the wheelbarrow nearby filled with potatoes that dad had brought from the cellar. The sun would be warm on her, filling her body with a dreamy content and making her mind quiet and full of the peace of a spring day.

And now today, the little purple sprouts on the potatoes bring it all back to me again: the holes being dug in the good brown earth; children with pails of the cut potatoes walking along the rows, dropping them, three to each hole; dad following with the hoe, covering them quickly to hide them from the sun, patting the soil down, moving from end to end of the garden; all of us together working in unity of purpose, my mother sitting on her up-turned box singing softly to herself, little Gaelic songs that her mother had sung in the green meadows of Ireland, and perhaps all the mothers of her race had sung as they cut the wrinkled potatoes for the planting.

Dusk would creep in on us before we were finished and the barns would look warm and homey and seem to huddle closer together for companionship against the coming night.

Then the planting would be finished at last, the pails gathered and set against the house. Dad would scrape the hoe and let it lean against the house too, and we'd all go in with tired feet and backs but gladness in our hearts and the smell of earth upon our clothes and hands.

CHAPTER 24

"Thankful
For What"

I think it was always there, the poetry, deep inside me, struggling to get out. I could feel it in my head like a tiny radio set waiting for someone to turn the dial and let it sing. Other times I would feel it just above the pit of my stomach, a kind of sick feeling as if you were in love and didn't know what ailed you. Other times, it was more of a golden ecstacy.

Once, I wrote a poem when this golden feeling came upon me in the midst of a domestic upheaval with everyone around me quarreling; we were moving and everything was uncomfortable and cold and unlovely. Then it happened. I was standing in the middle of the kitchen when the glow appeared and I seemed somehow to be alone there; the noises and confusion died away and I walked into my mother's bedroom where the sewing machine stood with the leaf down, and wrote the poem as fast as my hand could move across the paper. There was no hesitation, just the quick moving hand and the voice saying:

THANKFUL FOR WHAT

Not for the mighty world oh Lord tonight,
    Nations and kingdoms in their fearful might,
Let me be glad the kettle gently sings,
    Let us be thankful just for little things.

Thankful for simple food and supper spread,
    Thankful for shelter and a warm clean bed,
For little joyful feet that gladly run
    To welcome me when the day's work is done.

Thankful for friends who share my joy and mirth,
    Glad for the warm sweet fragrance of the earth,
For golden pools of sunlight on the floor,
    For peace that bends above my cottage door.

For little friendly days that slip away
    With only meals and bed and work and play,
A rocking chair and kindly firelight
    For little things . . . let us be glad tonight.

There it is, just as it came to me.

I sent it to *Good Housekeeping* and they used it in the November, 1932 issue and had their own artist make a drawing to suit the poem. After this it was sent out to newspapers all across the U.S.; they claimed it reached a million homes. It was later chosen as the outstanding poem of the year by the *New York Times*.

I think my mother was more excited over this than anything I ever did, before or since. She took the magazine to the Ladies Aid and passed it around and everyone praised it to my blushing face. One kindly neighbor said, "Isn't it nice to have a thing like that happen to one of our own." I received twenty dollars for it.

In my early days writing paper was very scarce. A new scribbler was prized beyond words; a new pencil was a gift from the gods. To this day I cannot bear to see beautiful white paper wasted. When I see anyone take a whole sheet of smooth lovely paper to write an address on or scribble a few words, I almost cry out, "Oh, don't do that!"

It wasn't that my parents were either stingy or poor. Kids just didn't ask for things and I think I was especially timid even for a child of seventy years ago. I am sure my father would have brought me a scribbler from Moose Jaw if he had known how badly I wanted one. Remember, we were twenty-five miles from town and kids wrote on slates in those days. Later, of course, I graduated to the use of scribblers which I still use. I have fifty-six of them, the thick ten cent size, crammed full of poems written on every subject under the sun from a clothesline full of nice clean clothes to the coronation of the queen.

I might say here that fifty years later, these scribblers have been sent to the archives in Saskatoon. I knew I should put them away for safe keeping; one day recently, I received a phone call telling me that R. H. Macdonald of *The Western Producer* in Saskatoon was coming down to get them. He flew to Toronto, and with the help of Sandy Nicholson, M.L.A., who originally suggested the plan, and a Toronto lawyer, we had the scribblers sent away in a fireproof trunk to the archives at Saskatoon; now my mind is at rest, for I always worried that something might happen to the scribblers and we would lose them. There are about 3,000 poems, common, ordinary poems, telling about life in Canada and especially on the prairies. I am glad too, for no child will ever grow up in the pioneer conditions that we did and so much of what we experienced might be lost forever.

CHAPTER 25

About
Books

My first little books were published in 1932 and after I received my copies I didn't sleep for three nights. Mr. Miller, the editor of the Moose Jaw *Times Herald* who had bought my early verse and had given me encouragement when I was young, had come to the office where I was working in Victoria, Scurrahs Ltd., and said he thought it was time I had a book of verse published. He asked me to choose thirty-five or so of my best poems and let the *Times Herald* publish them.

So I chose enough for two small booklets, giving them the titles of *Wide Horizons* and *Drifting Soil*. They were to sell for twenty-five cents each. The *Times Herald* printed 10,000 and in less than two months they were sold out. They printed another 10,000 and they too sold like hot cakes. I think the secret of their success was their size. They were small enough to fit into an ordinary envelope and hundreds of women bought them as little gifts for friends, instead of greeting cards. (I might mention here that this past summer, 1976, the Moose Jaw Library paid sixty dollars for one of them in order to make their collection complete, and to honor Mr. Miller who started the whole thing.)

Again, my good friend Mr. Miller showed his fine generosity and gave them to me at five cents a copy, exactly what it cost the *Times* to print them. By selling them at twenty-five cents I made a nice little profit, the first easy money I had ever earned in my life and I felt like a queen.

Then the Toronto publishers began to take notice and in 1935, Thomas Allen Publishing Company came to me and wanted to print a larger book to sell for one dollar, and asked if I would be interested.

I was definitely interested, and so a book was published entitled *My Kitchen Window,* with a foreword by my dear friend Nellie McClung. The book contained seventy-five poems. The jacket was bright and pretty with a red geranium on a window sill. It was an instant success and sold all across Canada and is still selling, although copies are hard to find as Thomas Allen has gone out of business and no more books are available.

Dreams In Your Heart came next, then *Beside Still Waters, Roses In December, Aunt Hattie's Place, Backdoor Neighbors, Hills of Home, Fireside Poems,* and the last one in 1953, *Golden Road.* I still get a thrill when a new one comes out, spend a couple of sleepless nights over it, carry it around with me to show anyone who will look at it. Like the man at home who had seventeen kids, the last one is always the best.

All in all, they have sold over a quarter of a million copies. I have written around 3,000; I've never had time to count them; of these, not quite 1,000 have been published in book form.

After the poetry, comes the fan mail from every corner of the globe. Recently, I received a letter from Africa, from a young married woman desperately homesick for her mother in Toronto.

During the war a young airman somewhere in the Mediterranean wrote to tell me that his mother had sent him my poem on the Church of the Redeemer in Toronto, and he was so excited because he had been a choirboy there. He said, "Gee, it made me feel homesick and sort of nice all at once."

I also got a letter from three soldiers in a fox hole in Italy telling me to keep on writing the poems, because, they said, "Miss Jaques, you kind of write about the things we're fighting for in this hell hole — love and peace, good grub on the table, kids and bicycles, and oh, all the lovely things, that you don't see here."

A sailor on the high seas told me that my poem, which he found accidentally in an old *Toronto Star,* gave him courage. For he said, "You see I am not sure of my girl, but I know I have to believe in her; and so your poem, 'You Have to Believe in Happiness,' hit the nail right on the head."

A priest in the high arctic wrote to say, "Since I read your poems I understand myself better and will carry on."

A young war bride said, "Thanks for your poem," that touched her heart.

> I just keep hopin' foolish like
> That you will come along,
> That I shall see your face again,
> And hear your happy song.

A farm woman wrote shyly for a book, telling me that her husband thought she was crazy to spend good money for poetry when she could spend it for something that would show up more.

Two letters from Buckingham Palace and a nice friendly note from Mrs. Eisenhower are lovely praise for anyone.

Editors of smaller places published my poems too, from Yellow Knife to Newfoundland, from Fort St. John to Kamloops and Vancouver and Regina, and small newspapers that you never see outside their own villages and little towns.

Sometimes I get a dollar for them, sometimes five, and now and then, ten. One of them, "In Flanders Now," reprinted in the United States, made more than a million dollars for women's clubs who made a little booklet with the Belgium national anthem and flag on it, that sold for ten cents. They used the money for the restoration of the national library in Brussels. I got about forty dollars out of it, all told.

CHAPTER 26

Surprise Parties

In the early years, nearly all of the homesteaders were young married couples with one or two children; in the wintertime when there was little work to do they would get bored to death. Then someone would plan a surprise party, go on horseback around the neighborhood and tell everyone to come to a party at someone's house, usually ours, as my mother loved company and was a good entertainer and most important we had a piano. Not that they needed entertaining; just being together to talk and listen was enough to make them happy.

Because dad was the oldest family man in the settlement (he was just thirty-seven), it usually fell to our lot to be the place where the party was held; and we all liked surprises.

As a rule they would meet at someone's house and all come together in a big sleigh, drive quietly into the yard and then all at once let out a warwhoop that would deafen a horse; amid laughter and hellos they would pile into the house and start to have fun.

After the horses were put in the barn, the men would come into the house and start to throw out the furniture, all except the stove, and the way would be cleared for a good old square dance. Someone would run over to grandad's and get them to come over. Grandpa would bring his fiddle (that his family had brought from the old country a hundred years before), and he would perch himself on a stool in the corner of the room, start to saw away and the dance was on.

There was no classical slow dance music for him; he played all the old favorites by ear: "Turkey In The Straw," "Irish Wash Woman," "Money Musk," "Comin' Through The Rye." How they all danced in that tiny room, I do not know. But the fun went on as they bumped into each other, laughing; dipping and swaying and kicking up their heels, they would stop to pant and get a drink of water, and start again.

The babies would have been put away upstairs on the bed, and younger ones would sit on the stairs with us; I don't know who enjoyed it the most, the dancers or the spectators.

Around midnight, the coffee pot would be put on and the lunches unpacked (that they had brought). Salmon sandwiches were the favorite, along with angel cakes and cookies. There was never any drinking; my mother would have scalped anyone who dared bring a bottle or a deck of cards into the house; they were the Devil's tools, she would say.

After lunch the babies would be brought downstairs, rosy and smiling, and the older children would be wrapped up to their very eyes, and the party was over.

Then they would all join hands making a circle in the little room and sing, "Should auld acquaintance be forgot, and never brought to mind ...", grandad playing it on his violin and all the people singing.

Then we would stand outside and watch them go, hearing the sleigh bells getting fainter and fainter, falling into the eternal silence that even to this day hangs above the lonely prairie giving an eerie feeling, as if the earth had just been finished and was still half-asleep.

• • •

The winter of 1906-07 was one of the coldest and snowiest winters ever recorded in Saskatchewan. The first blizzard came about the middle of October and it hardly let up day or night until spring. But one day it eased off a bit, and what did we see coming along the trail from the west but a sleigh with a team of horses and two young men in it.

They drove into the yard, and my father and brothers went out, and before they could say they couldn't stay, my father had the horses in the barn and we had them in the house, and my mother was getting a meal on the table. Before we finished eating, a beautiful blizzard had come up and kept them there for three days and nights.

They were good singers and good talkers — how we enjoyed them; just to hear a different voice raised in laughter was balm to our lonely hearts. I don't think we ever stopped laughing and singing and telling stories.

When the storm stopped the third day, they hitched up and went on their way and we never saw them again; but my sister and I have loved them all our lives.

CHAPTER 27

Lodge
Night

There was one night in the month that we could count on dad being away: lodge night. The Masons got one started in Drinkwater. How we looked forward to it, from one month to the next.

My dad was a stay-at-home man, who never ventured out after dark if he could possibly help it. Living on the farm, naturally the only real warm place we could gather was in the big kitchen with its old black cast iron stove, belching warmth across the room with now and then a gleam in the lamplight from the nickel ornaments on the oven door, the warming shelf at the top, and the teakettle that sat toward the back of the stove and sang a little tune to itself, purring like a kitten in the warmth and cheer.

Most nights dad would be safely ensconced in his red armchair, reading the weekly newspaper, the Almanac, and now then a book.

My mother would be reading too. She always had one tucked in under her pillow for safe keeping during the day and she'd bring it out at night and sit in her rocking chair, reading and muttering to herself, now and then grunting with disgust at something in the book.

But lodge night was different. Dad would start to primp for it about four o'clock in the afternoon, shaving, changing his shirt, combing his moustache, putting on his good shoes, and telling mother to hurry with supper — he didn't want to be late.

We three girls would eye him impatiently; all we wanted was to get rid of him and start to enjoy ourselves, which we couldn't do if he was sitting there watching, which he always seemed to be doing.

At last supper would be over and dad away in the red sleigh to Drinkwater, about ten miles away. Out would come the pan to make taffy in. Then would come the corn popper and the deep pan to soak maw's feet (she always had about a dozen corns, callouses, and bent toenails to be fixed up.) How we enjoyed it, the peace of the kitchen, the gentle purring of the teakettle, my sister Madge "doing" maw's feet, the old dog snoring behind the stove, letting out an occasional yelp at something in his dream.

After the feet were fixed up, my mother would get sleepy and say she was going to bed, and we'd be left alone in the kitchen. Maybe we would read for a while, then decide to go to bed too. And in less than an hour, the old house would be still; a wall board or stair might creak a bit, but there was always that sense of peace and security there as we crept into bed and said our prayers; in ten minutes we would be asleep. Never in all the years since have I felt that golden sense of security and hominess that I felt in that old home.

CHAPTER 28

Sweet
Sixteen

I was growing up, although I never did get very big: five feet high and weighing about 100 pounds was about all I ever got. My sisters were small too, and I don't know why; maw was a nice plump 5' 5", dad was about 5' 8", and Bruce was a six-footer.

The young people would gather in the schoolhouse on Sunday evenings and talk and laugh together. Then there would be a short service with someone reading a little story; we would sing a couple of hymns, and the rest of the evening was spent getting acquainted with each other, as this was the only way we could ever meet any young people.

Dad used to call it a courting school, but if it was, where could you find a better place to meet a nice, decent boy, look him over, and make your choice. For believe me, the girls had the choosing, and many nice loving marriages were started here; many of their descendants are still there, happy people whose roots are in the fine decent soil of that little new settlement.

I had my eye on one of them; he would come up to me after the young people's meeting and pull my hair or pretend to push me off the school desk where the girls would perch; my heart would give an extra thump and I'd be happy for a week. I didn't get him. A nice girl from Ontario came out to keep house for her brother and she won his heart. Maybe she had more practice than I had. I think they were happy enough. They had a pretty little girl who moved away after her parents died, as they both died fairly young.

As I said, 1906 will go down as the winter of the big blizzard. Nothing before or since has equalled the terrible fury of the storm that hit the country. It was a beautiful sunny morning and I said to my mother I would like to go and visit the Elliots, and she said, "Well, go ahead. They'll be glad to see you." So I went on horseback with the dog, Toots, following me at a nice distance for fear she would be sent back as she hated to be separated from me. I think in her faithful way she thought she was taking care of me (or maybe it was the horse); anyway, she came along, trotting quietly behind with her head down.

Mr. and Mrs. Elliot were glad to see us. They were friendly people, laughed easily, and Mrs. Elliot was the best cook in the country.

The sun was still shining as we sat down for dinner, but it wasn't long before Mr. Elliot said, "Say, did you hear that funny sound like a ghost or someone shrieking up in the sky?" And then it hit. In less than ten minutes the world we knew was shut out by whirling snow driven by a gale-force wind; the barn and other buildings were completely shut out. A weird sort of darkness came down on us with shrieking winds like banshees screaming in the sky. As old Bill said, "All hell broke loose," only it was a cold hell, the likes of which we had never seen before.

Toots crept close to me, keeping her nose on my foot as if for comfort, shivering too from the weird shrieking of the wind.

For three days and nights it kept up. Mr. Elliot never went to the barn. His wife said to him, "You better go and feed the horses," and being Bill he said, "The hell with them. They had better die than me." So we all stayed close. Luckily they had just got a ton of coal, and the coal bin was against the house, so we were never in danger of freezing.

My dog never left my side. Once Mrs. Elliot in fun gave me a little slap, and Toots was at her like a flash, snarling and growling with bared teeth. She followed us into the little bedroom at night where I slept with Mrs. Elliot (Bill had the sofa), went around to the side I was lying on and slept there all night long, alert for trouble, nervous and on edge, sensing danger but not sure just what it was.

The third morning dawned bright and beautiful on a world of frozen whiteness. Drifts twenty feet high were piled up wherever you looked, hard as rock, as if mountains had been moved. Mountains of snow, decorated with millions of diamonds, sparkled wherever you looked. My horse walked on top of the drifts that were packed as hard as ice, but I can tell you I rode carefully, and the horse seemed to know that he had to watch his step too or we might all be swallowed in an icy drift.

When I was about halfway home I met my brother Bruce coming for me, walking. My mother had been in agony for three days wondering if I had started out when we saw the storm coming. My faithful dog crawled in behind the cookstove in her old familiar spot and you could hardly get her out of the house for a week.

Our barn was completely covered. Dad and the boys had to dig a tunnel fifty feet in to where they figured the door would be, and let the horses out. They seemed dazed and almost blind from the utter darkness of the barn for three days.

Dad dug out the hen house door and threw the hens out onto the snow. They too were blind from the darkness, but as he threw them they started to fly and hit the side of the granary and fell against it; but, they soon recovered and started to gobble up the wheat he threw in a little cleared space, while my sisters and I sat on top of the snowdrift and laughed at their antics.

Thousands of cattle and horses were lost in that blizzard, from Saskatchewan to Alberta. The cattle had stampeded when the blizzard started and piled up on top of each other, and died by the hundreds. Men caught on the trail just died on their sleighs, or were found frozen stiff under them where they had crawled for shelter.

A neighbor of ours got off his horse and was found beside a haystack frozen stiff just as he sat crouched in his overcoat. Another poor homesteader was found hugging a post, maybe hanging on to it for comfort; he just sank down exhausted and froze to death. Some of the people were never found until spring, but the coyotes had got there first and there was nothing left but bones and a ragged piece of overcoat or pants; and that is how they identified some of them. More than likely the horses would be found, frozen stiff, still hitched to their sleighs, with only bones and bits of harness to identify their poor remains.

CHAPTER 29

Hauling
Wheat

Money was scarce and wheat had to be hauled to Drinkwater (after an elevator was built). It was a long haul for most farmers. We were the closest and it was ten miles each way; that is a long way when the thermometer hits forty below.

They would load their sleighs the night before, then get up around five a.m., feed the horses, get breakfast, put on all clothes they could pile into, and start out. As every trail in the whole country passed through our yard, they would follow each other to Drinkwater, one team behind the other. I have counted forty sleighs at one time, snaking their way across the white earth, most of the men walking behind their sleighs, climbing on now and then for a rest, then walking a mile or so again. They looked like one long brown snake wending its way across the flats.

After they unloaded their wheat at the elevators, they would go to the little hotel and have a huge dinner of good prairie beef, potatoes, vegetable and pie — always pie — and coffee.

Then there was the long trek home; sometimes it would be almost dark when they got there. My mother used to hang a lantern on the corner of the house, or set a lamp near the window, afraid someone would get lost or a horse would play out on the trail and they would need help. Years after I wrote this poem:

LAMPS

I love old lamps that shed their light
    Like golden aerials
Across the lonely prairie night,
    To homesick neighbor souls.

I love old lamps, their steady glow
    Across the kitchen clean,
They seem to stand for us somehow,
    The best that Life could mean.

And no road ever seemed so long
    If I could look and see
Across the lonely prairie night,
    The lamp set out for me.

And though the aching years divide
    Old things serene and sweet
Across the years their beauty shines,
    A lamp unto my feet.

After supper the sleighs would be loaded again, ready for the next morning and another freezing trip of twenty miles there and back — more, for people living farther away.

This would often last all winter, depending on the size of the crop. They never got a big price for the wheat either. I remember that when it finally hit a dollar a bushel, they thought they were millionaires.

When I was around sixteen I sold a couple of poems to Billy Sunday for a mere pittance. He was the noted American evangelist of his day. My poems were set to music and sung at his meetings. Twenty years after I came across one of them in a hymn book and could hardly believe my eyes.

Around that time I won first prize in a poetry contest sponsored by a tailoring firm starting up in Regina. The prize was a man's suit of clothes. I was ashamed to tell my family that I had won it, but was afraid I'd be put in jail if I didn't accept it. I finally got up enough courage to show them the letter and was surprised to find that they were proud of me. Dad bought the suit from me and gave me twenty dollars for it, which in those days was a small fortune.

How do the poems come to me? I do not know. I just don't know. Even in those early years the little verses would form in my mind, as if a voice were softly saying them to me. It's hard to explain, but they were there, singing:

> My dreams are little windows
>   Where I can look and see,
> A golden ship all laden
>   With lovely things for me.
>
> My dreams are rainbows shining
>   When stormy clouds are gone,
> A bow of promise given,
>   The silver pledge of dawn.

Or a poem on September:

> Oh moon of falling leaves . . . Oh golden hour
>   The purple grape, the aster for thy dower,
> The warm sweet scented sheaves all bound and tied,
>   The amber haze that fills the countryside.

• • •

How I wanted a desk. I asked for one timidly (kids didn't demand things in those days.) But I never got one. Looking back, I think not getting one was one of the biggest disappointments of my life.

But I found a big wooden box, set it up in the corner of the attic, and wrote my faltering verse on it. No one ever disturbed my 'poet's corner', although they all thought I was crazy.

CHAPTER 30

The First
Wedding

The first wedding in our family was that of my oldest brother, Bruce; the lovely bride was Jean Hughes, a girl who lived next door to us in Collingwood, who had come out to teach school. Her first school was at Lumsden. She had come to visit us one Christmas and was told that she could get a job in the little Sunnyhill school about a mile from us.

So the next year up she came, boarded with us and what on earth could be easier than falling in love with the oldest son of the house. We all liked her and that made it easier.

Bruce built a little house about a quarter of a mile from us, painted it green, and there they set up housekeeping, happy and carefree as the birds in the air.

They were married in the parsonage in Drinkwater. We all went in our usual high style with a team and a sleigh. How young and unafraid they were, the two of them, standing before the minister, taking their vows to love, cherish and protect so long as they both should live; for once we younger ones were subdued, watching and listening, sensing something we hadn't known before — the sacredness of marriage, and the promises of love.

Then we all drove home, after throwing the traditional rice all over the preacher's carpet. My mother had a lovely supper ready for us. We sang a few songs, and then they walked home, across the road, looking lonely and small, in the white moonlight, like pilgrims starting out for some promised land, beyond the rainbow's end.

CHAPTER 31

The
Store

Somewhere around 1905 or 1906, dad got another idea: he would build a store. It was a good idea as some of the homesteaders had to drive from ten to twenty-five miles to buy their groceries. He said he always had wanted to be a storekeeper anyway, and this was his chance.

So he built a store, about twenty-by-forty feet, and stocked it with everything anyone could think of, and a lot of other things some of them had never seen in their lives. At one end was the little post office, moved from their bedroom to the store, a more respectable place he thought.

They built a long counter, rows and rows of shelves and left the back part for bags of flour, 100 pound bags of sugar and the vinegar barrel. It was a success from the start. Now the women could come and do their shopping, and talk and laugh and get their mail.

The men liked it too, for sometimes trying to get their groceries when they were drawing wheat was a sorry job; and most of the time they would forget the most important thing on the list, such as yeast or salt or baking powder, and when you were twenty miles from town, it was a disaster.

We enjoyed it too. I loved meeting people, writing their grocery list on the little counter checkbooks and talking to them, hearing about their troubles and pleasures, warming them up if it was wintertime. I don't know why we didn't give them a cup of tea now and then; it never entered our heads to do so, but I know it would have cheered them up to sit down with a nice hot drink and cookie while we filled out their grocery list.

A lot of the groceries were bought on credit, and as dad was a poor collector, hating to dun anyone, I know (for I kept the books) that hundreds of dollars are still owing for goods bought sixty years ago.

Dad always gave big measures. I think I let a few extra ounces slide off the sugar scoop too, as we talked and laughed with the customers.

I can remember most of the prices after all these years. I can see them on their shelves: one pound tins of baking powder, twenty cents; sugar, five cents a pound; raisins, ten cents a pound; currants, ten cents a pound; pickles (the big gallon jars), ninety cents; beautiful red salmon (the big cans), twenty-five cents a can; flour (Robin Hood), $3.25 for 100 pounds; coal oil, forty cents a gallon; royal yeast, ten cents a package; chocolate bars, five cents.

They would load their groceries in boxes and go home knowing that, for a couple of weeks anyway, they could cook good meals.

No one bought meat. Each family would have a prime steer fattening up, five or six pigs, turkeys, chickens, ducks, and sometimes, if they were from England, they would have a couple of sheep to kill in the fall.

And with twenty-five or thirty bushels of potatoes in the cellar, turnips, onions, carrots, and maybe a few cucumbers and ripe tomatoes (if the frost didn't come too early), everyone lived like kings, fattening up on the best food in the world; most people were content and satisfied with their lots in life with no bosses over them and their horizons as wide as the sweep of the sky that flowed with the sunrise and sunset to the rim of the world — and beyond.

We kept the store until the railroad came in 1911; then, naturally, people went to town for their groceries and the little country store at old Briercrest just folded up and died.

A relative, Herb White from Collingwood, came out and built a fine store in the little new town and the little store building on the farm was cut in half. One part was moved to town and is the post office today, still carrying its store front and sound as the day it was built. And to add to the history of it, a Jaques is the postmaster.

The other half of the store was moved back a bit and served as a bunk-house for the hired men after Bruce and Clyde had gone their separate ways.

In the fall, the hired man was moved into the house to a little bedroom off the kitchen that was warm and not so lonely. Then my mother would go out and start cleaning out the bunk-house. She would dismantle the bed, and stand it up against the wall, scrub it within an inch of its life, as she said; then she would put in a couple of saw-horses and boxes, lay new boards on them that would serve as a refrigerator for the meat all winter. That refrigerator was the coldest one you ever felt.

And what meat is was. I'd love to have a slice of her homemade headcheese, or liver loaf. A steer would be killed and cut into roasts and steaks and stew meat. A couple of pigs would be killed and treated the same, and perhaps a few turkeys and chickens as well. It's miracle we didn't get sick. I guess we ran it off and were as healthy as calves in a stall.

Unexpected company was no problem; there was always plenty of food in the pantry, or bunk-house. I pity anyone who never knew the abundance of those early years, or the utter peace of a prairie night in the winter with the moonlight molten silver and maybe the howl of a coyote sounding like the wail of the dead shattering the stillness, and then letting it come back again in little echoes that beat against your ears and made you half afraid.

CHAPTER 32

The First
Baby

Charlie, the first baby, came along just fifteen months after the wedding, right on time, squalling and wiggling, and scaring his father to death. He made such hideous faces, Bruce thought he was some sort of monstrosity; never having seen a new-born baby before, he nearly fainted, rushed downstairs, fell over a chair, swore, and started to cry.

Then he went back upstairs where the old midwife was making Jean comfortable and my brother took the new baby downstairs; the baby was clad only in a teddy bear blanket. Somehow or other Bruce managed to get some warm water in the wash basin and bathed the baby, put his little shirt on backwards, wrapped him up again, laid him in a bread pan and held him close to the open oven door as he was shivering with the cold, his little jaws hunting even then for his first meal.

My sister, Madge, and I were so anxious to see him that we got up at 2 a.m., although a ground blizzard was blowing. When we opened the door, there they were, Bruce holding Charlie quietly and singing "Annie Laurie" to him, with a look of wonderment and joy on his face that this small bit of humanity was really his son, born in a blizzard and destined to go his lonely way to an early grave, with no son of his own to carry his name into the next generation.

I'll never forget how my dad loved Charlie. Jean would bundle him up and walk across to our place for the day when Bruce was away with grain. Dad would unwrap him, lay his things on a chair, pick him up; then he'd start to walk the floor with him, back and forth across the kitchen, singing, and the baby would lie there content, knowing, I am sure, that he was safe and loved and he had come to the right place.

After him, three fine boys were born, tall, nice-looking young men. Charlie, the first one, died in his forties. Howard, the next one, was a rear gunner on a plane in the war. One night, returning to England from a bombing mission over Germany, three enemy planes tried to run them down. He used to tell us how they would cross back and forth behind his plane shooting at them, and by the time they got to England, there was hardly anything left in the rear of the plane but him, sitting with his feet dangling; they had hit everything but him. One bullet cut the leather of his wrist watch and his precious watch, a gift from his dad when he enlisted, dropped into the English Channel; but, he came home without a scratch on him. Such is fate, I suppose. The other son, John, got his wings on his eighteenth birthday and they told him he was the youngest flyer ever to get wings, as they couldn't get them until they were eighteen.

He flew his bomber too, all through the war and came home still laughing as when he went away. He came back to his little home town of Briercrest and swears it is the loveliest place in the world and he asks nothing better than to live there, and be buried in the little cemetery south of the town. I hope he gets his wish.

He married the only girl he ever went with, Ruth Tisdale, a neighbor's daughter, whose grandfather was one of the early settlers, and all her kith and kin live on nearby farms. John runs the oil business and is known and loved within a twenty mile circle of the town.

Bruce had always wanted a daughter and his wife had gone to Regina to wait its arrival. When the phone rang about midnight and he was told that a girl had been born, he just sat in his armchair in front of the stove and muttered to me, "It's a girl."

After sitting there he leaped into the air, kicked over the coal scuttle, laughed like a hyena, ran out into the yard, did a couple of loops, came back, and cried a few tears of pure happiness and went to bed; and next morning he was still so happy about it that I didn't know what to say to cool him down.

All in all, they had the four boys and two girls and all are doing fine, I am happy to say.

CHAPTER 33

Washday

Washday really started the day before. Dad, or whoever was handy, would load a barrel on the stone boat and hitch up Old Farmer (the steady horse), and with a couple of pails, would head for the pond, accompanied by three kids and a couple of excited dogs, who ran ahead wagging their tails and barking their pleasure at the whole expedition.

The banks of the pond or dug-out were steep and always slippery, with that oily, black slipperiness of prairie mud of the worst variety. Now and then a kid would slide down into the water and stop the whole project while someone fished him out and sent him or her bawling back to the house and mother.

When the barrel was a good three-quarters full (dad cussing most of the time at the inconvenience of having to haul water up in the pails slipping and sliding up the banks), Old Farmer was told to "git apt" and the stone boat would slide along the short grass to the back door of the kitchen. The barrel would be left standing on the stone boat, while mother would come out with a can of lye and put about four dessert spoons of it into the water to settle and soften it.

Next morning, the water would be clear as crystal and quite soft. The boiler would be put on the stove and half-filled the minute breakfast was over; a bar of good yellow soap would be shaved off to melt and make suds.

The washing machine (if you were lucky enough to have one) was then hauled in from the porch, and the dirty clothes were sorted while the heated water from the boiler poured in and the work really started.

Our washing machine was operated by hand. A handle would turn the thing inside round and round and often the clothes came out "whiter than white," as they say on the television advertisements now; the glow would begin to show on my mother's face.

On the other side of the kitchen (we had a big one) was a two-way stand for tubs for rinsing and blueing the clothes. The wringer was on a heavy upright between the two tubs and the work of putting them through the wringer usually fell to me.

Then the clothes were put into a clothes basket and taken out into the yard where the clothesline ran between the corner of the house and the corner of a smaller house about 100 feet away.

If it was a windy day, there was a struggle to get them on the line. If it was a good hot drying day, the first clothes put out would sometimes be bone dry by the time you got to the little house at the far end of the line, and then you'd go back and start all over again.

This all sounds simple, but it wasn't. As a rule, water was precious and so washday just came once a week and there would be lots of clothes. By noon though, we would be nearly finished with the washing.

Then, after supper, would come the cleaning up. Ashes were taken out, coal brought in, the floor scrubbed, kindling split and laid behind the stove, supper made and dishes washed and put away.

By this time everyone would be tired. Maw would sit with her feet in a pan of hot water and Epsom salts. Dad would be reading the *Family Herald;* the kids would be reading or drawing. The dog would be asleep behind the stove, while the cats dozed on mats.

The setting sun would throw a glow over our world; there was peace and contentment that modern living does not know — a sense of home, just plain home, in the farm house with its outside buildings clustered around as if they needed the blessed closeness of us human beings against the bigness of the oncoming night.

By nine o'clock everyone was in bed. We didn't need sleeping pills to make us sleep — we were dead the minute we hit the pillow, dad snoring, my mother coughing a bit.

We three little girls would be in one big bed, curled around each other like kittens, warm and content and healthy.

Outside, the night was filled with tiny sounds, the stomping of feet in the barn, the low moo of a cow in the corral, a night bird off somewhere in the dusk, a coyote calling across the flats, stars as big as teacups holding the sky up like a tent.

CHAPTER 34

"Man With
A Lantern"

I was staying with Clyde and his family on the old farm one winter after my parents had moved to town. Bruce had gone to town and I knew he would be bringing the mail home; so after supper I said, "I'll run over and see if there was anything for us."

As I was walking over, just before going into the house, I saw Bruce coming around the end of the barn with a sheaf of oats under each arm, and carrying the lantern with him. Suddenly this poem came to me, just as if it had been waiting for me to see him. I ran into the house and yelled to my sister-in-law, "Get me a pencil, quick, and a paper." She rushed around looking for it and the only thing she could find was the empty cover of the writing pad. So she handed me that and I got the poem, without a break, complete and finished. It is now used in our Canadian readers and I was delighted to learn a few years ago that it is used in the readers in Scotland. Here it is:

MAN WITH A LANTERN

He moves within a ragged patch of light
    Doing his chores about the stable way,
A blot of dancing yellow in the night
    As back and forth he goes for sheaves and hay.

Whistling he moves about his humble chores,
    The friendly stock and stable warm and dim,

Long moving shadows play about the floors,
    The horses softly neigh for oats to him.

The cattle stand beside the stanchions bare
    Yielding their snowy milk, its fragrant heat
Rises like incense on the frosty air,
    The bedding straw is gold beneath their feet.

A kitten rubs its face against his arm
    Purring its friendly trust, the dog is close
Wagging his stubby tail in happy charm,
    His master's love the only heaven he knows.

Ah could you find more gracious life than this,
    Full days of toil and lovely brooding night,
Good food and love ... and windows through a mist
    And homes within a yellow patch of light.

CHAPTER 35

The Second
Wedding

The second wedding in the family was that of Clyde to a lovely Scotch girl, Mary Boan. Her parents had come out from Inverness, Scotland in the early eighties and Mrs. Boan was pregnant. The baby was born at sea and only lived a few days. Mrs. Boan never got over the tragedy of having her baby buried at sea; sure, there was a church service, and they let her come up on deck to see the tiny box lowered and given to the sea. The passengers tried to comfort her, but to her dying day she never got over the fact that her baby was put into the cold stormy Atlantic.

They settled in the Qu'Appelle valley, when Moose Jaw was the end of steel. There were only a few white families; all the rest were Indians, resentful of people coming and taking their hunting ground away and forbidding them to carry guns in the little village.

They had to go to Moose Jaw for groceries. The winter trips were awful; getting lost in a blizzard was a constant fear, so they moved to Moose Jaw where he set up a lime kiln. After a few years of this he came to Briercrest district and bought a farm near the hills. By this time the family had grown to twelve; four girls, eight boys. The boys were all over six feet tall, good workers, clean living, bent on making a living on the farm.

My brother had his eye set on Mary, the oldest girl, with her rosy Scotch complexion, lovely blue eyes and sunny golden hair; he didn't lose any time in letting her know how he felt.

They were married in April, right there in her home, and what a lovely wedding it was. Mrs. Boan had cooked enough food to feed an army, the table was set in the dining room and the wedding took place in the big living room. I was supposed to play the wedding march. I had been practicing it for weeks and knew it by heart, but when they came slowly into the room, Clyde's face was whiter than anything I had ever seen in my life — he was whiter than a ghost, and walked like a man in a trance. Looking at him, I forgot the wedding march entirely. I think I wound up playing "God Save The Queen," but I am sure no one, let alone Clyde, even heard me. He managed somehow to grasp what the minister was saying and answered the right words and they were declared "man and wife," promising to love and cherish each other till death should them part. The vow was kept for over fifty happy years.

At the wedding supper with all its bounty, I don't believe Clyde uttered a word and he still stayed as white as a sheet. Mary did her best, but we were all glad when the meal was finished and the horse and buggy were at the door waiting to take them to their little house on the farm dad had bought for him about six miles south of us.

Their little family came along too; the first one was a tiny baby girl. Mary came to our place to have the baby and the night the baby started to come, Madge and I stood out in the yard crying. We couldn't stand the inside of the house with Mary screaming, Clyde whiter than a sheet, and maw giving her a whiff of chloroform now and then to ease the pain.

After it was born, I think the best looking one of the lot was Mary herself, lying high on her pillow, rosy cheeked, and happy it was all over.

A boy came next, then two more girls and then last, but not least, a nice gentle boy that the dad almost worshipped; that special love lasted as long as Clyde lived. And so the second generation of the family, rooted in the rich soil of Saskatchewan, is still there, proud to be numbered as descendants of the first pioneer of the Briercrest district.

CHAPTER 36

Mother

I think the kitchen is the nicest room in the house, especially if it is bright and cheerful and full of color. I remember our old kitchen. At first it was a dull tan color with brown woodwork. It would give you the blues even on the nicest day in the summer. In winter it would drive you crazy with the dark walls staring down at you and making the early twilight just that much earlier and duller looking.

Then one day (long before home and garden magazines came along to make us wise) my mother got the idea of brightening up the kitchen. My father hooted at the idea. Weren't the walls nice and serviceable, didn't show the dirt or fly specks, and a calendar here and there was all the color it needed — so dad thought.

But she got out the catalogue and ordered some bright flowery wallpaper, pinks and blues and greens, and bright turquoise blue paint for the window sills and doors, then sat back and trembled at her audacity, wondering if it really would look nice when it was done.

She needn't have had any doubt. When the wallpaper came, it was even nicer than it looked in the catalogue; when we got in on, and the woodwork painted, and new dotted curtains on the windows, you just couldn't believe the change it made.

For one thing, the kitchen looked twice as big. The walls were clean and shining, even the furniture seemed nicer and the old cookstove that had been blackened within an inch of its life, fairly glowed with good cheer and solid comfort.

We didn't have cupboards and counters in those days; we had a pantry, and after seeing how pretty the kitchen looked, my mother thinned out the rest of the paint and worked on the shelves in the pantry and put new newspapers on and you never saw such a change as it made either. She even painted the old brown flower pots and made them new and cheery looking.

In the kitchen was a long table to accommodate seven family members, two hired men and any visitors who might come along. The sewing machine stood beside the east window and was always open with some bit of sewing on it. There was a wash bench behind the kitchen door with an oilcloth cover and little curtains to hide the old shoes and rubbers underneath.

FARM KITCHENS AT NIGHT

The kettle sings a low contented tune,
    The dog snores in his sleep behind the stove,
There is a mingled odor in the air,
    Of apple pie — of cinnamon and clove,
The smell of yeast — for mother set the bread
    In the blue pan before she went to bed.

An old gray cat is sleeping on a chair,
    Paws folded in below her snowy chest
She looks the picture of contented peace,
    Like an old lady waiting for a guest,
Her eyes blink softly as if half-awake,
    Pale green like water in a mountain lake.

The kitchen has a fragrance of its own,
    Of porridge simmering in a blue pot,
Of kindling wood drying beneath the stove,
    And red coals glowing beautiful and hot,
There is a sense of joy and comfort there,
    In the old stove and cushioned rocking chair.

A feel of home and peace and fireglow,
That lovely modern kitchens do not know.

We always took a weekly newspaper and farm magazine. The *Family Herald and Weekly Star* was daily reading and from it anyone would get a good sound education and be up on the world affairs. To my father's dying day you couldn't talk about anything in the world that he didn't know something about.

My mother too, loved the printed word and had a reverence for it that almost amounted to foolishness. I can remember her calloused hand caressing the covers of a book as if she loved the very feel of it, touching the letters of the title and the author's name.

She read everything she could lay her hands on and near the last, when the tide of life was running out, she had been reading the poems of her beloved Tennyson:

For such a tide as moving seems asleep
    Too full for sound or foam,
When that which drew from out the boundless Deep
    Turns again home.

She was a wonderful woman. Even today, when I too am old, I marvel at her wonderful spirit; no matter what crazy thing we tried to do, she helped whenever she could. She never had much money. Dad saw to that, and kept the purse strings tightly tied. But she always had a few dollars to hand out when the need arose.

She would go into her little cubby hole under the stairs, dig down in a trunk and come up with the money we needed. It wasn't much; we girls got along with almost nothing and made our own clothes; a few yards of nice new print or muslin, bought at the local store, would keep us happy for the summer.

She would sit in her old rocking chair, rocking and singing old Gaelic songs; we couldn't understand a word she said, but we liked to hear her sing, with her eyes shut and kind of smiling, as she sang.

She said her mother used to sing them when she was a child and she didn't understand them either, but liked the sound of the words and the wailing tunes that went with them that made you think of banshees crying across the bog in the dead of night.

• • •

There is no surer or more welcome sign of spring than the seed catalogue. How my mother loved them. The day the Mackenzie seed catalogue arrived from Brandon, I can tell you that for one night at least, she didn't go to bed at nine o'clock.

We would get the supper things put away in record time, then she would sit at one end of the table where the lamp was, and read every page of it, as excited as if she had discovered gold. There she would sit, picking out the seeds she would need for her garden; no flowers were ever sweeter than the ones pictured there: shamrocks, carnations, nasturtiums. She would rub her hand over the pages, and read them from cover to cover. A new variety of flower was as important to her as a new star in the heavens.

But she never had much success with them. The prairies are wind-swept and we never had any kind of a windbreak around the garden. There would be colored pictures of carrots and peas, and lovely tomatoes growing up against a wall, and cucumbers in little round beds; she could almost taste them. I don't know why, but her efforts were so often in vain. After she died, I found a Bible and a seed catalogue under her pillow, with a leaf turned down here and there where she was no doubt planning to get a new flower or vine. She had the most success with sweet peas; they seemed to stand up better to the wind, and somehow she always managed to string a bit of page wire to give them a little protection. Years after I wrote this poem for her, as if in thanks to a catalogue:

TO A SEED MERCHANT

Your catalogue arrived today,
 Thanks for its cover bright and gay
And all the lovely host it brought,
 Delphiniums, forget-me-not,

Nasturtiums clustered to one side
   And pale pink roses for a bride.

Although the winter wind is blowing,
   Here in my room are flowers growing,
Petunias in their gay attire
   And marigolds like sacred fire,
With canterbury bells to ring
   Above the tender fields of spring.

Outside my window blizzards rage
   But here upon the glowing page
They smile like lovely guests — and oh,
   I am so glad that flowers grow
In books. I have them twice you see,
   Next summer in my yard . . . and here tonight
Before the fire with me.

● ● ●

I was in Lethbridge when Clyde phoned me to hurry home because she was going fast. I took the next train and he met me at Moose Jaw and we drove out to Briercrest. When I saw her dear face I knew the end was near.

The next week we spent the most of our time together. She would laugh at old memories and I would laugh too, with a lump in my throat.

Late one afternoon we knew the end was near; we phoned both of the boys and they came in. Bruce sat on the edge of her bed holding her hand, his tears slowly dropping down. Dad couldn't stand any more, so he rushed out into the living room. Clyde stood near the bed, beside me.

She opened her eyes and smiled at me and said: "When you think I am going, be sure and open the door. I could never get out through those three little holes in the storm window."

And then it came — no struggle or sound, the quiet breathing stopped. I rushed to open the door and called "goodbye maw" and waved her on her way and I'll never forget the glorious sunset — all gold and the tiny clouds fringed with yellow and rose, with arrows of light pointing upward into the blue.

It was March 5, 1938. She was seventy-six years old.

She was buried in Briercrest and afterwards I found beneath her pillow a little red leather book of the Four Gospels and a tiny envelope with a quarter in it, her next month's dues for the Ladies Aid. Nearby lay the seed catalogue.

In 1902, the author and her family left this house in Collingwood, Ontario, to move to a homestead southeast of Moose Jaw, Saskatchewan.

The author's brother, Bruce Jaques, was photographed in 1909 in one of the first Model-T Fords.

The Jaques family's first car was preserved for posterity in this 1911 photograph.

The Jaques' homestead house, 14x20 feet, was located twenty-five miles southwest of Moose Jaw, Saskatchewan.

This is the only available photograph of the author's parents, Charles Jaques and Nellie O'Donohue Jaques.

Charles Jaques, the author's father who sailed the Great Lakes. was captain of this boat, The Mona, *in the late 1920s and 1930s, sailing on Buffalo Pound Lake in Saskatchewan.*

The author became a "sailor" for a year and is pictured on the Princess Adelaide.

This picture was taken in Calgary, Alberta, in 1919 when the author took her first flight in an aircraft. The top of her head is visible as she sits waiting for the pilot to prepare for take-off.

This photograph was taken around 1925 when the author was living on a homestead in Barford, Saskatchewan.

Edna Jaques and her daughter, Joyce, were photographed in 1940 as they posed in front of the grandparents' home in Collingwood, Ontario.

This photograph of Nellie McClung was taken in 1934 on her property near Victoria, B.C.

In 1966 Edna Jaques visited the Egyptian pyramids. (She is pictured in the upper right-hand corner.)

Edna Jaques is shown enjoying the Flanders poppies she got from Nellie McClung's garden in Victoria, where they had been brought after the First World War.

Edna Jaques poses for this photograph taken several years ago in the yard of her daughter Joyce's home in Willowdale, Ontario.

Edna Jaques poses with her daughter, Joyce, at a party celebrating the author's eighty-fifth birthday. The photo was taken in Joyce's home in Willowdale, Ontario, where the author lives.

The hollyhocks in the photograph grew from seed the author brought home from the Holy Land. Her "Holy Land Hollyhocks" were sent to her friends all over Canada.

CHAPTER 37

Changes

Often the children on these isolated homesteads would be terribly lonely, especially if there was only one child and no school within ten miles. Now and then a father, drawing wheat to Drinkwater, would wrap up a kid and bring him or her as far as our place to spend the day with us, warning the child to be good.

For the first half-hour he or she would sit primly on a chair watching us play at whatever we were doing, but soon the child would be up and whooping and hollering with us, almost beside itself with happiness to be playing with someone.

There was one little girl who lived down near the hills, the most beautiful child I have ever seen. Now and then her father would bring her with him, and apologetically and with smiles, land her at our back door, peel off her coat, and tell her to be a good girl.

She was painfully shy, but soon got over it and when her dad came for her around five in the afternoon she would cry and beg to stay. My mother always had a little treat wrapped up to give her at the parting, maybe a little cookie man, a little loaf of bread or a tiny pie just for herself.

• • •

By 1906 or so most of the homesteads were taken up. The C.P.R. had been given one section in every seven as payment for building the railroad. Most of them had been sold to the new settlers, some of whom put up signs across the trails, reading "no roads any more". How we hated those signs. I remember the first one I saw; it was at the south side of our place, right across the little trail we used to go south to Gallaughers or anyone living south of us; as well, it was the trail to the hills.

When I came upon it, I nearly fell off my horse; it was just a little piece of new board that said "no trail". I couldn't believe my eyes. Even my father hated the square fields, the straight graded roads and fences and the look of civilization that was beginning to take shape before our eyes.

We wanted the country as it was, rough and wild and untamed. We wanted to be able to get on a horse and wander where we liked, but deep in our hearts we knew the old order was giving away to new, and there wasn't a thing we could do about it.

CHAPTER 38

Threshing
Time

Threshing time was the highlight of the year. How we children would thrill and run around the yard in circles as the great steam engine came panting and snorting into the yard, belching fire and smoke and hauling its equally big and cumbersome separator. Dogs would bark and the cows gallop to the farthest end of the pasture, there to watch in terrified fascination as the machine was spotted where they wanted it; then the golden stream of straw would begin to hurtle through the air into a pile that would soon become a straw stack, fragrant as a bed of pine.

The quiet yard would become a place of feverish activity, of wagons and hayracks, horses, yelping men and dogs, kids and half the neighbors.

My mother enjoyed cooking for them. Many women dreaded the coming of the threshers, but not her. She loved to feed people and here was plenty for her to feed, the hungriest, most ravenous people I ever saw eat.

What roasts she cooked, what mountains of potatoes and turnips and parsnips and homemade pickles. She made the most delicious meat pies I've ever eaten. She made them in a blue granite milk pan, and the men's eyes would fairly pop when they'd come in and see her table set. "Boys," they'd shout, "let's stay here until Christmas."

For that matter we lived like kings all the time.

Dad would kill a steer in the fall and a couple of pigs. My mother always had a nice flock of turkeys, and thought no more of killing them than I would think of frying a pork chop today. There were always chickens galore, fresh eggs, our own cream and milk and vegetables. We didn't know it then, but during those years I was to know the best food of my lifetime — the very best.

CHAPTER 39

Keeping
Company

As I said before, in 1911 the C.N.R. came through our district connecting Moose Jaw and Radville, and shattered forever our small and narrow world. It brought strange people and trade from the far corners of the earth, prospectors and carpenters, a blacksmith shop and a livery stable, two new stores, and a bank. More exciting than all the rest, it brought in new men and boys who wore white shirts every day of the week and Sunday suits, and who tipped their hats to us as they went by. I grew up the winter after the railroad came.

The next few years were the happiest and most carefree of my life. Boys and dances, the new church, and new friends filled our days to overflowing. The Jaques girls didn't know it then, but they were having the time of their lives.

We had a good home and parents who drove us with an easy rein. The house was filled with company. After the lonely years my father and mother were hungry for people. Sundays, the yard would be filled with buggies, with horses tied to the hitching posts, the stable overflowing. Two good-looking older brothers brought the girls flocking to visit the Jaques girls, and plenty of free and wonderful grub brought the men like bees to a bag of sugar.

During this time I was still writing bits of verse here and there, putting them together lovingly, taking them out to read and change and ponder over, never forgetting even in the excitement of the new world we had entered that they were there, like a secret love, warming my heart and claiming my loyalty.

Once Bruce took me aside and said kindly, "I want to tell you something. Don't talk to anyone about your poems or show them to our friends. We like them you know, because we like you — but outsiders will think you are crazy. They'll laugh at you."

Again I took my troubles to Mr. Miller, my good editor in Moose Jaw. He walked the floor a few minutes and then turned eagerly to me and said, "What if they do laugh at you, what if they do — let them." And he added quietly, as if to himself, "They'll change their tune someday." Then he said, "Could you do me a poem a week? We can't pay you much but do you think you could do it?" I promised fearfully to try and in this way I began to drill myself into some sort of discipline. He got his poem a week and I got a dollar and a half for every one he printed.

Then the editor of the *Saskatchewan Farmer,* Harry Cook, wrote to ask me if I could do two a month for that magazine at the same price. Again, I said I'd try. I don't believe I missed an issue in nearly thirty years, and although other editors have come and gone, they still get them and publish them in their magazine that comes out twice a month, and I still get the same price we started out with — a dollar fifty per poem. It all comes in handy.

Then the *Free Press* of Winnipeg came up with another request. Did I think I could do a poem a day for them. By this time I had begun to feel my oats and rashly said I would. I kept it up for seven months and then begged off. I could do it all right, but it was worrying me, and besides it took up too much of my precious time; I still wanted to play.

For it seemed suddenly as if our world was overflowing with men, while girls were scarce as hen's teeth. At the dances the men outnumbered the girls about five to one. When the caller-off announced the next dance, there was such a stampede for the girls that often a wave of real fear would come over us that we might be trampled in the fray.

It wasn't that any of us were so good-looking; there just weren't enough girls, and if a boy wanted to dance, he had to get there first. What square dances we had — what fun — what laughter! Sometimes the music would be just the local boys playing a violin or accordion or, in a pinch, a couple of mouth organs — it didn't make the slightest difference to us. We were young and full of life and drunk with the magic of youth.

You might be going with a bank boy one night, and the kid from the next farm the next night, or someone entirely new who had caught your eye for the time being. Looking back I marvel at how nice they all were. There was no drinking in those days at the dances, absolutely none. I remember just once an older man had asked me for a dance and not knowing how to refuse I danced with him. Suddenly I smelled liquor on his breath and began to tremble. I left him standing in the middle of the floor and went over to Bruce, who was sitting on a bench alongside, and sobbed that I was afraid of him. Without a word my brother walked over to him and told him quietly that the best thing he could do was to get out, and he went without any argument at all.

Looking back, too, I think the thing I remember most was our laughter. My sisters and I would laugh at the drop of a hat. We laughed and sang and danced and wore out our slippers gliding over the rough new floors that had hardly been laid before we danced upon them. The girls would bring sandwiches and cake and the boys would give the musicians a few dollars and everyone was happy. Often a whole family would come in a bobsleigh. The older women would make the coffee while the babies slept peacefully in a corner of the room rolled up in their blankets, dead to the world. To this day the smell of coffee and salmon sandwiches bring a lump into my throat for the old happiness that we once knew.

I think that during this time I was always in love, but not with any one boy in particular. I liked them all and blithely went with one and another as the days went by. There was a red-cheeked bank clerk from Aberdeen whom we called Scotty, a young newcomer from the States, a neighbor lad who danced well, the new hardware man, a couple of Mounties, a clerk in a store, a tall rancher from the hills, a dark boy from the Maritimes, a scarred veteran of the Boer War. As long as they could dance without walking on my feet, I loved them all, or thought I did.

And then one day the real one came along. We didn't even know his name, but my sister and I were walking up the new plank sidewalk of the little new town of Briercrest and as the stranger passed us he took off his hat and said gaily, "Hello, girls," and went on his way. I said to my sister Arlie, "Oh, I think he's wonderful. Did you see how beautifully he took off his hat to us — like a knight with plumes. I think I'll marry him."

My sister wasn't quite so smitten. "You're crazy," she said. "Why, he wouldn't marry you. You don't know half as much as he does. Why, he might be from Ontario."

I found out later that same week that his name was Ernest Jamieson and he was from Ontario and was the new owner of the harness and leather shop and one of the most eligible bachelors in town.

After meeting him, I would give him a special smile at the dances and gradually we started to "keep company". He would hire a horse and buggy at the livery stable and drive out and I would sit upstairs on the bed looking up the road that he would take coming from town; my heart would start to beat a little faster as he got nearer the house. Then, likely as not, a sudden fit of shyness would seize me and I wouldn't come downstairs until my mother would call up, "Come on down Edna, Jimmy is here." How I loved it, coming down and meeting his nice smile with the whole family looking on. I would hardly say a word through supper, or until the family made a diplomatic exit to their rooms in order to let us have the kitchen to ourselves.

Then I would lose my shyness a bit and talk a blue streak more than likely, with my feet propped up on the oven door and him sitting in front of the stove, warm and comfortable. I would watch the clock, for he had to go at ten, no later; at ten he would get his overcoat on and go home.

CHAPTER 40

Dorothy

Early in 1914 an English family by the name of Christy moved to Briercrest. He was middle-aged, she in her thirties. He was a carpenter, built himself a small house and went to work, made friends and settled into the life of the small town.

In November a little girl was born to them: Dorothy; two years after, the little mother gave birth to a nice baby boy. It was a hard birth, and there was no doctor, no nurse, no hospital — only an old mid-wife who was all right if everything went well. In this case things didn't go right, and a few minutes after the baby was born the little mother just shut her eyes and quietly died, poor little thing.

A woman out near the hills by the name of Barnard adopted the new baby, but the father didn't want to part with the little girl, who by then was a sweet little curly-haired kid with a happy laugh and cute ways; so he refused to let anyone have her.

He would give her her breakfast, put her in her play pen near the window with toys and leave her while he went to work. Sometimes, lonely at night, he would go out for a game with the boys and she would be left alone at night also.

A neighbor tried to keep an eye on her, but as winter was coming on, she worried for fear he might not come home and the baby would freeze to death in the shack; so she sent for the mounted police to Avonlea. He came up and they had a trial. It seems you just can't take a child from any parent without just cause and there must be a proper trial.

So a trial was called; attending were the justice of the peace, the Mountie and a few onlookers. Mr. Christy appealed to them to let her stay with him, but the Mountie said to dad, "I won't leave her with him; the only way I'll leave her is for him to get her put some place where there is a woman or some girls." So dad said, "Well, we'll take her out to the farm, for the time being. He'll likely get married again and then he can have her back."

So the next day, Madge and I were sent to town to get her with a horse and buggy. When we drove up to the house, he brought her out wrapped in an old brown shawl. She had no coat so we set her between us on the buggy seat and took her home.

She was a sweet little thing and when she was brought into the kitchen with her little straw suitcase, she went and sat on it. And after a while I took her upstairs to the girls' room where there were two beds and a little cot; she became part of the Jaques' household from that day on, and fitted in like the last part of a crossword puzzle.

Her father stayed around Briercrest for a couple of years. We had him out on a Sunday to see her, but he got lonely I guess, and one day he just took the train and we never saw him again. We heard years after that he died in an old folks' home in Moose Jaw.

So as the years went by and our family got married and went their ways, Dorothy was a great comfort to my mother. She did small chores around the place, went to school, brought in the eggs, fed the hens, ran little errands to my brother's place; later, when maw and dad moved to town, she went with them and went to high school, and was always a help and comfort to my mother in her old age.

When I moved to Victoria, I sent money for her to come out, got her a job, and about a year after she married her boss, went home to England with him where he was drafted into the army and sent to North Africa. He was shot walking up the beach from the landing scow; he never made it to land. He was brought back and died in hospital in Newcastle and she was left with a two-year-old girl. She also had a son a few weeks after

Alf died, born under a steel table in a hospital, in the middle of an air raid on the dock side there, in Newcastle.

She married again and he died also. But she managed to raise her two children, and they are fine decent people, both managing somehow to be happy and good in spite of the unhappiness behind them; both came back to Canada to live.

Last summer, the mother, Dorothy, came out for a visit and we had a lovely party for them; I never saw such happiness and laughter, as that day. It was a joy to watch them, having mounted the hurdle of the hard years to meet again with no bitterness toward God or man for their hard upward climb.

She lived in damp cellars, shabby cold rooms, attics and dumps, but never became resentful or hard. Recently, she wrote me she is getting an apartment for her retirement and I sent her some money to help with the furnishings; she is buying a carpet for her little flat and is happy.

CHAPTER 41

Calgary

My sister and I would drive to town in our new buggy, walk around, talk and giggle and speak to everyone we met, for indeed we knew most of the people for ten miles around, and it wasn't like going to a strange place and having to get acquainted.

I would dart into the harness shop to have a few words with Jimmy, enough to make me happy for a week. There was no talk of marriage, although most of my friends had settled down and were having babies. I remember one special friend, Kitty Fraser, whom I had known since she was ten years old, married a neighbor and had a baby in due time. When we went to see her with her new baby, I just couldn't believe that Kitty, my friend, had a baby. It didn't seem possible, but there he was, fat and rosy and her nursing him.

Jimmy, for some reason or other, was kind of shy of the word "marriage". Maybe he wanted to have a little more fling or hated the thought of tying himself to any one woman.

How decent everything was; there were lovely dances in the dining room of the new hotel, or in Whites Hall over the store, or in a nice hall above the pool room, with sandwiches and cake the girls had brought. Coffee was made on the cookstove of the couple living in two rooms at the front. How homey and safe it all was — a lot of good clean fun with square dances, waltzes and two-steps, and lots of laughter.

After about three years of this, when Jimmy really was "the one" in my thought, I got tired of it and said to my mother,

"I think I'll go out to the coast for a trip. I can work my way from town to town, sewing." She started to cry and asked me fearfully if I thought I could take care of myself. I assured her I could, and one bright morning I took the local train to Moose Jaw and was on my way.

I stopped off at Calgary, looked up the help wanted ads and applied for a job in the sewing room of the Holy Cross Hospital, sewing. There were five or six girls, a half-dozen sewing machines, and we had a wonderful time. It's so easy to be carefree when you are young.

A little nun presided over us and I got to love her very much. She was French and pretty. She would sit near a long table and sew and cut out pillowcases and sheets and bed pads. She didn't say much, but I know she listened to every word we said and enjoyed it, although the mother superior scolded her now and then for enjoying us. It was all good girlish fun.

CHAPTER 42

"In Flanders Now"

Our whole family loved poetry. Even Clyde was known to have written the odd poem and Bruce, although a rather grim man, wrote me a poem of welcome when I visited them on one of my trips west.

I can remember my grandmother Jaques in her "outside" rocking chair, reciting poems to us, rocking back and forth with her eyes shut and enjoying herself, as well as entertaining us.

My sister Madge let me read a few of her nice little poems and Arlie, the youngest, still writes a poem now and then for her own enjoyment. So poetry was a "natural" for me.

When Colonel McCrae's immortal poem, "In Flanders Fields", was printed, I memorized it; then, one day in the sewing room of the hospital, the "answer" came to me like a flash of lightning. I screamed to the girl next to me in the sewing room, "Give me a pencil quick, and paper." She dug a pencil out of her purse and said, "I haven't any paper." I looked frantically around for paper but there was none there. So I turned over a spool box (thread used to come a dozen spools to a box) and on the back of it I wrote my answer to his poem, as fast as my hands could write it, no thinking, no pausing, just the words coming in as if someone were saying them. Here it is:

IN FLANDERS NOW

We have kept faith ye Flanders dead,
  Sleep well beneath the poppies red
That mark your place,
  The torch your dying hands did throw
We held it high before the foe
  And answered bitter blow for blow
In Flanders fields.

And where your hero's blood was spilled
  The guns are now forever stilled
And silent grown,
  There is no moaning of the slain
There is no cry of tortured pain
  And blood will never flow again
In Flanders fields.

Forever holy in our sight
  Will be those crosses gleaming white
That guard your sleep
  Rest you to peace the task is done
The fight you left us we have won,
  And peace on earth had just begun
In Flanders now.

One of the highlights of my life came unexpectedly in connection with this poem over fifty years later. I was in Ottawa and went up to Parliament Hill to attend the memorial service for the war dead and veterans on November 11. It was a beautiful autumn day, warm for November and hundreds of people were gathered near the eternal flame waiting for the arrival of Governor General Roland Michener, to begin the service.

When he arrived precisely at eleven o'clock, there was a hush on the great crowd who had come for the service. He gave a fine speech in his usual dignified manner, and then said, "And for the closing of this service, I will read Edna Jaques's poem, the answer to Colonel McCrae's immortal poem, 'In Flanders Fields'. Here is her poem." As he read on and finished the poem

I just sat there on a bench — I was too far gone to stand — shut my eyes and thanked God up there in the sky for the honor of letting me be the one, in all of Canada, to write the answer to Colonel McCrae's poem, voicing for all time our thanks to him for his poem written on the back of a dirty envelope, as he gazed over a graveyard in France where the scarlet poppies were blowing in the wind above the sleeping soldiers.

Long years after, I was speaking at a club in Toronto and an elderly man stood up right in the middle of my talk, pointed his finger at me and said, "Did you really write the 'answer' on the bottom of a spool box?" and when I said, "Yes," he said, "Well do you know, I was with Colonel McCrae in France when he wrote 'Flanders Fields'. We were standing together looking over a huge graveyard, and he pulled out a dirty envelope and wrote his Flanders poem on the back of it." Strange how both the first poem and the answer came like a flash and were written on the first things we could get our hands on — a dirty envelope and the bottom of a spool box.

I had rented a typewriter from a business college so I could practice typing in the evenings; that night I typed the poem and sent it to the Calgary *Herald*. A couple of days after, I received a letter from the editor, Mr. Wodell, asking me to come and see him. So on my next day off I went to the *Herald* building, found his room, knocked, and when he yelled, "Come in," I went in. He looked up kind of mad and said, "What do you want?" I whispered, "I am Edna Jaques." He yelled, "My God," and told me to sit down.

He couldn't believe that the thin shy little person was really the Edna Jaques who had written the poem. But after assuring him that I was, he printed the poem in the *Herald*.

Shortly after that, the U.S. newspapers took it up and syndicated it in hundreds of papers. Then Everywoman's Club in Washington had it printed on a little folder, with the picture of the Louvain Library in Brussels that had been bombed. They sent them to Everywoman's Clubs in the U.S. and made over a million dollars and used it to restore the library. Mrs. Percy Pennybaker, who was president of the national clubs, wrote me claiming that an American woman wrote it.

It was used in the ceremony in the chapel of the Arlington

Cemetery near Washington when they brought back the first "Unknown Soldier". My uncle, John Jaques, was at the service and he spoke to the minister and pointing to the poster at the front of the altar said, "My niece wrote that poem." The minister replied, "Rubbish, an American woman wrote it." And Uncle John said, "Well, there is her name, Edna Jaques, and I am John Jaques." The minister just walked away.

That beautiful poster now hangs in the chapel with my name on it, and they still claim that an American woman wrote the poem.

After that, Mr. and Mrs. Wodell sort of "took me up", invited me to their home, and encouraged me to keep on writing; they were my most loyal fans as long as they lived.

Then, one day, I suddenly got tired of the sewing room and everyone in it. So down I went to my good editor of the *Herald.* I said, "I'm tired of sewing," and he said, "What would you like to do?" I said, "There are two things. I would like a ride in an aeroplane (wild wish) and then go to Vancouver." He smiled his nice smile and said, "Well my dear, I'll give you both your wishes. I'll arrange a plane trip with Captain McCall, and I'll fix up a pass for you to Vancouver." He then added timidly, "Do you think you could write a poem up in the air?" And with my usual stupidity, I said, "Sure."

The war was over and Colonel McCall had just come home from flying his little plane, fighting in the air and doing a fine job of it, and was giving ten minute flights to anyone who was crazy enough to take a ride, "barnstorming", they called it.

It seems incredible now, less than sixty years after, that great planes carrying 200 and 300 people can fly over oceans in a few hours. You can eat and sleep or read the newspaper in peace, with only the quiet purring, or breathing, of the engines to tell you that you are ten miles up. And even the Rockies look like little hills and hummocks below you, if you can see them at all.

When I got back to my room I sat on the floor (I don't know why I chose the floor,) and imagined myself up in the air, and wrote the first poem on the sensation or feeling of being up in the air, then memorized it and after the little flight of maybe fifteen minutes, went back to the *Herald* and typed it out to the amazement of my good editor. (I hope in heaven, he does not read this.)

It was printed in the paper next day. I am sure my editor would forgive me for saying I wrote it in the air; I was too scared to take a long breath all the while we were up. But I have a nice picture of myself, sitting on the wing of the plane (the plane not much bigger than a hay rack) wearing pants and putties, and a middy. This old picture was shown at the air show in Ottawa the summer of 1974, and a friend told me that all who looked at it laughed their heads off.

THE TRAIL OF THE AIR

Poised for the flight with its far flung wings,
And the throb of its eager heart,
With a whir of motors and belts and things,
See our bird of strange plumage start.

Borne on its breast like a gull we rise,
On its mighty wings we go,
Cleaving the fathomless depths of the sky,
While the world drops down below.

There's a singing wind and a rushing sound,
As the day grows red in the west,
And quickly we drop to the quiet ground,
Like a homing bird to its nest.

But we have tasted the sky's vast depth,
Have breathed of its sun and rain,
And into our hearts has the rapture crept
From the wings of an aeroplane.

There were ten verses altogether. Imagine writing them in my room, then memorizing them and telling my editor that I wrote it "upstairs". Knowing him, I know he'll think it was great.

CHAPTER 43

I Become
A Sailor

A few days after this I boarded the train for Vancouver, and like the Israelites of old, not knowing whither they went, I arrived in the biggest city I had ever been in, and went to the Y.W.C.A. where I got a room, and didn't know what I would do next.

But on the train, sitting across the aisle from me, were a mother and her young daughter. We talked back and forth and they too went to stay at the "Y".

I had told them how I was looking forward to my first view of the ocean and next morning we three went down to the dock. I asked them to take my arm and lead me down the last block with my eyes shut, so the glory of the sea might burst on me all at once, which they laughingly did. When we were about halfway down, they said, "Now you can open your eyes," and what did I see: the great harbor as far as you could see from either side, one mass of ships, big ocean liners, coastal steamers, little fishing boats, all white and glinting in the sun, as if in answer to my wildest dream. And before me there was a blue sparkling sea, a thousand times more beautiful that I had ever imagined it.

I thanked them and went back to the Y.W.C.A. and said to the woman at the desk, "Oh, I wish I was a boy and then I could work on a boat." She said, "Well, you know, you don't have to be a boy now; there is one boat, the *Princess Adelaide,* that is hiring girls. There's a strike on and they are using girls."

I said goodbye and started on the run back to the dock,

down the sloping run to the ship. There was a man standing there, a tall nice looking man, and I said, "I hear you are hiring girls to work on the boat." And he said, "We are." I gasped out, "Will you take me?" He laughed and said, "I will you Irish giant. . . . Can you be back in a half-hour?" I yelled, "Sure," and ran back to the Y.W.C.A., got my grip and started on the run. I didn't know enough to take a street car. I arrived just as the whistle blew, and Mr. Allen smiled and said, "On with you. One of the girls will tell you where to go." Thus began the happiest year of my life.

It was called the "triangle run" — Vancouver, Victoria and Seattle — six days a week. We left Vancouver around 10:30 a.m., went to Victoria sailing through one of the most beautiful seas in the world, through the "narrows" — the boat would rock in the meetings of the tides — around little stormy islands. Sometimes it seemed we would almost hit them, but the stout little ship with Captain Hunter standing staunch as a soldier in his little glassed-in lookout, giving his orders to the men far below, eased along with hardly a ripple, until we came around the last bend and headed into the open sea to Victoria.

There were fourteen of us, nice decent girls. They had partitioned off the rear end of the lower deck with a huge canvas for us, just above the propeller rod. Sometimes in the night on the run from Seattle to Vancouver, I would wake up to the steady beating of the propeller quietly turning and driving us along. It sounded soothing, like a heart beating in the night.

Each girl had a narrow cot, a little bureau and a rack for her clothes. Here we could wash out small underclothing, iron our uniforms, put our hair in curlers. We were safe and protected, and if Bill, the night watchman, had ever caught a curious passenger trying to get a glimpse of us through a slit in the canvas, Bill would have thrown him overboard, I am sure.

How we enjoyed it, the companionship and the comfort, the happy laughter that always seemed to be there. I never met a nicer lot of girls and Captain Hunter was proud as a peacock of us; in a kind of fatherly way, he took care of us all.

Each girl had eight staterooms to make up every morning. For me, being short, making those upper berths was surely hard. Now and then a tall girl would give me a hand, but as a rule I stood on a chair to make them up and as far as I know there were no complaints.

Each girl had her table also, where we waited on about eight people three times a day. How we stood it, I will never know. We worked fifteen hours a day, ate three big meals, slept the minute we hit the pillow and were happy as clams.

The officers of the ship treated us like they would their own daughters. We always had that sense of protection and good will, and the atmosphere of the ship was, strangely enough, a family affair.

We were all proud of our captain. He was a tall nice-looking Scotsman with rosy cheeks. When he would appear at the dining room for dinner in his fine uniform with his cap in his hand, a little hush would come over the whole dining room as he walked with dignity to his place at the head of the captain's table. The other officers would rise and stand as he came in and took his place, and then sit down and proceed with their meal, talking easily but with a bit of restraint.

Even the passengers would stop eating and watch as he came in; we girls would, almost unconsciously, stand straight behind the chairs until he was seated — a little act of respect that we felt toward the master of his ship of which we were so proud.

We would serve dinner from about five to eight and arrive in Seattle at nine p.m. Sometimes, when there wouldn't be too many passengers, we would finish early, and in order to fill in an hour or so until time to dock, a few of us younger girls would gather on the lower deck at the back and begin to sing. Maybe two or three baggage boys would join us. One of them had a guitar and as the boat moved along in the still moonlight, there would be a lovely air of happiness among us, with the beauty of the night and the long swells of the sea as it rolled in from deep water and struck the high white cliffs of Washington.

I can remember the cliffs as the moonlight hit them, shining and white against the darkness of the sea and sky, and then we would feel the quiet slowing down of the propellers as we came closer in. Then would come the shouting and running feet and the crew getting ready to unload; the spell would be broken, and work started again.

After an hour-and-a-half in Seattle, we would go down to our "glory hole", slip into our cots and be asleep in five minutes, safe and warm and strangely at home as the boat plowed its way back to its home port of Vancouver.

The girls were as varied as life itself, something like a "sample" picked out from the patterns of time. One was a little Scotch war widow with two little girls that a relative kept for her up near Nanaimo, B.C. Another was a war widow from London, whose husband was killed on the Marne; she found it hard to keep a smile on her face, but did pretty good. She would invite me now and then to go home with her for a weekend, where she had a sister living in the west end of Victoria.

One was a red-haired girl about sixteen who sang like a lark. She would yell hello to the boys whose ships were tied up at the dock not far away — ships from China or Japan — and they would shout something back to her in Japanese and she'd laugh as if she understood what they said.

Mrs. May, the older woman, was from Calgary. She was a war widow too, and was trying to bring up two little girls and having a hard time of it.

A couple of the older girls chummed together and didn't have much to do with the rest of us, but were friendly in a way; they would sometimes pass around a box of candy that a passenger had given them instead of a tip.

It was for the most part fun, and as I look back on that time of my life I have a nice feeling toward them all. I'm glad that for a short time in my life I was a sailor.

One morning a curious thing happened. As we usually tied up at the Vancouver dock around 8 a.m., many of the passengers went down and had breakfast before leaving the boat, and we girls who cleaned the rooms got an early start on our work. That morning I noticed one of my rooms had been vacated and I went in and started to clean up, strip the bed, and tidy things up. Then I noticed some rings in the wash basin and on the stand and even on the floor, so I picked them all up and could hardly believe my eyes — diamonds, rubies, emeralds, pearls, ten beautiful rings worth a king's ransom.

Then in order to keep them safe, I put them on my hands — even the thumbs — and went on with my work until I could finish and take them to the purser. Presently one of the girls came to me and said, "You are wanted in the purser's office. The captain and first mate are there, the chief and the purser, and a woman raising Cain. Gee kid, have you done anything wrong?" I laughed and said, "Well, no," and with a light heart I went along with her to the office. In order not to make them laugh at me, I clasped my hands behind my back, as I went in.

Captain Hunter looked at me in his kindly way and said, "I believe you look after room 121." And I said, "Yes." "Well," he said gently, "Did you see any rings there?" So with a little laugh I said, "Sure, here they are," and spread my hands out before him, every finger glittering with a priceless ring.

There was a gasp of amazement from everyone, then a snicker from a couple of the office clerks which the captain silenced with a lift of his hand. And he said to me, "Would you give them to me please?" I smiled and began taking the rings off and putting them in his hand while the angry woman looked on. Then he turned to her and said, "Here are your rings, madam, and I would advise you to take better care of your jewelry. And I would also ask you to leave my ship immediately." She left and went down the hall, kind of snorting and trying to explain why she had left her priceless rings in the wash basin and on the floor, and I went gaily back to my work.

It was the start of a nice ordinary day for me and everyone, and we had a good laugh at the look on the woman's face.

I stayed on the boat a year. As I look back I can see nothing but kindness, hard work, companionship and good money.

CHAPTER 44

Another
Wedding

Then my sailing life was over; my parents and two sisters came out to spend the winter in Victoria, rented a nice house on Fairview Avenue and I went to business college, one of the wisest things I ever did. When I finished and they had gone back to the prairie, I went over to see if I could get a job on the Vancouver *Sun Province.* Too stupid to know that a big newspaper didn't hire beginners, I went in boldly, asked the elevator man who was the big shot on the paper, and he told me it was Mr. Nichols. I looked until I found his door, knocked and went in; he growled, "What do you want?" I said timidly, "I want a job as a reporter." He said in a sort of sneering voice, "All right. Here is a nice new pencil; go out and get me a story." So I went out, walked the streets down to the dock again where I seemed to feel at home.

I couldn't find a story, and then cold and hungry I went back to the little dingy room I had rented and wrote a poem. Here it is:

> Have you seen the harbor lights,
>   Blossom in the Bay
> When the moon drops out to sea,
>   Out Victoria way.
>
> Have you seen the fishing boats,
>   Drift with tired sail,

To their quiet harbor place,
　　Down the sea's rough trail.

On the far horizon's rim
　　Phantom beams aglow,
Ghostly hulls of ships that sank,
　　Years and years ago.

Have you seen the harbor lights,
　　Blossom in the Bay,
When the moon drops to the sea,
　　Out Victoria way.

The next day I took it to him, and when he read it he gave one a rather puzzled look and said, "Well, you got yourself a job." For nearly twenty years the *Vancouver Province* used ten poems a month on the editorial page.

But the job was too lonely, so one day I packed my grip, bought a ticket for Moose Jaw (where my parents were living then), got into an upper berth and cried all the way to Moose Jaw. I arrived on a Friday night, went downtown next day and got a job in the advertising department in a big store there, Robinson MacBeans, and that was that.

I started work on Monday. At noon, walking up the street to a restaurant for lunch, who should be standing at the corner but Jimmy, smiling and looking beautiful. He held out his hand and as I took it he said gently, "Will you marry me?" And I said, "Yes," quietly, as if I had been waiting for the question, or it had been rehearsed before; maybe it was.

I worked until October and we were married on November 30, 1921, in the chapel of St. Andrew's Church in Moose Jaw, with only two or three friends, my father, two brothers and two sisters. My mother didn't come; she hated weddings.

We took the train to Regina, stayed for a few days at the Queen's Hotel. So started our married life.

When we came home and the train pulled into the little Briercrest station, there was a small crowd waiting to welcome us with laughter and confetti. Cec Windrum, the dray man, had backed up to the platform to get his load, but instead of that, they hustled and pushed us up on the dray, and we rode up the street, everyone laughing, storekeepers standing in their doorways waving at us, wishing us well.

Jimmy had bought some second-hand furniture from the relatives of an old couple who had died within a few weeks of each other. It included an old white bedroom set — bed, bureau and washstand — and for downstairs we had a set of dining room furniture that looked nice, a small table with two chairs for the kitchen, and an old stove that someone had thrown on the nuisance ground. But Jimmy had fixed it up and polished it within an inch of its life and I never had an oven that was a better baker in my life — and, it kept the downstairs nice and warm.

After that, we just naturally fitted into the quiet life of any prairie village in the twenties. Most of the men had small businesses — enough to make modest livings — rather small houses with nice gardens behind them, where we grew our own vegetables. Now and then the more ambitious grew small fruit. One woman was crazy enough (as the neighbors said) to try and grow apples, but she just laughed and went on with it and when I went home twenty years after I couldn't believe my eyes; her back yard was a wilderness of beautiful apple trees. I often wonder if they survived the long drought of the thirties.

Most of the people in the new village were young couples and babies were arriving almost every week. We would visit each other, bringing our babies that were admired and poked in the ribs, and as I look back, even the babies were happy and smiled at everyone who looked at them. Sometimes on the way to the Ladies Aid in the church basement, a half-dozen or more mothers would be pushing their go-carts up the street — a procession of them — laughing at each other, unwrapping the children when we got there, and they would sit on their mothers' laps and goo and squirm through the meeting as if they too were enjoying the company.

Most of the women just had their babies with the help of neighbors or their own families. But when I knew I was going to have one, I wanted to be near a doctor as I was nearly thirty years old and small, and just plain scared to have it alone.

A friend of my sister invited me to stay with them until the baby started to come, but they turned out to be unfriendly and I felt they wished they hadn't invited me. So one day when everyone was away, I packed my grip and started for the hospital, walking. It was about six blocks away and I had to walk in the middle of the road as the sidewalks were piled up with snow.

When I was about halfway there, I ran into a bunch of dogs who were fighting. I backed up toward the sidewalk trying to get away from them. A door opened and a woman came running out with a broom, waving it at the dogs who ran away. And she said, "Wait a minute until I get my coat and I'll go with you." So that is how I got to the hospital, walking with a strange woman helping me. How queer life is.

It was a small hospital with only a young nurse in charge, who couldn't have cared less whether I died or had the baby alone. Toward morning, another patient in the hospital called a doctor and when he came in, he said, "How long has she been like this?" And the nurse said, "Oh, six or seven hours." And he said, "Oh, goodness!" and clapped something over my nose; the next thing I knew it was night, when I heard a nurse say to another one, "Put the kid in with her and maybe she'll come to." Then someone laid a bundle beside me that squirmed and whined. I thought it was a puppy, opened my eyes, and saw a tiny baby face looking at me.

I shut my eyes, then opened them again and she was still there, and I knew it was my baby; such a wave of pure love swept over me that I nearly passed out again. And now, fifty years later, I still love her with all my heart, and will until the sod is laid over me.

Jimmy came up on the train the next day to see me. He came in smiling and happy, brought me a box of chocolates and a tiny rose bouquet for the baby, and was proud and happy as any new father is, with no thought of the long night's agony it had cost me to have her alone in a strange place.

Some of those babies turned out real winners in the wider world they went to when they grew up. Like hundreds of prairie villages and little towns, there was no work, no industry or places where a boy could grow into a job; so they "hit the rails" in the drought years and you could come across one of them in just about any corner of the world.

I remember once in England I dropped a penny on the floor. A man stooped to pick it up for me, and when he straightened up and handed it to me, I realized it was a kid from Briercrest, almost ready to cry with happiness to see someone from home.

Mrs. Greenwood, whose little boy was born the same week as my baby, would wheel him past our house and I would come out and we'd compare them. Mine was always fatter, but hers had a nice personality and would smile and wave at other kids passing. He is now president of the Bank of Commerce and has the same nice way with him that I remember as a little boy.

Stanley Glen, head librarian for the University of Toronto, is another kid from our small village; his sister, Blanche Glen, and her husband have been missionaries in Angola for nearly forty years.

My nephew, John Jaques, was the youngest airman in Canada to get his wings. He came home after the war the same good-natured person that went away, still laughing and pleasant. And he still thinks Briercrest is the nicest little place in Canada and wouldn't live anywhere else on earth.

CHAPTER 45

We Go
Broke

My husband's love for our baby was almost idolatrous. He was fine looking as they come, charming, and for the most part, easy to live with. But this love wasn't enough to make him work. He wouldn't work, just wouldn't. His sister said to me once, "Why did you marry? You knew he wouldn't work."

But I didn't know. All my men folk worked early and late. I was used to men who got up at five o'clock of a summer morning and were in the fields before seven with their teams, ready to start plowing. But Jimmy (my nickname for him) would stay in bed until noon and no pleas or threats or scolding would get him up.

Jimmy wasn't a drinker — he was just plain lazy. He loved to shoot the breeze. He was sociable and pleasant but he just would not work, either in his store or on the homestead.

He loved talking. As long as he had an audience he was happy — but that didn't put bread on the table or pay for the baby when she came. I paid for her from the savings I put aside when working before I was married. He would have been happy as an auctioneer or a travelling salesman — but he certainly was no provider.

With customers battling at the front door of the leather goods store and threatening to pull the place apart, he would snore peacefully away through the morning hours. Farmers coming in for repairs and oil and shoes would go away in disgust, and so the business went to the dogs.

A new thing was starting too. A farmer south of dad's place

bought a tractor run by gasoline. You could hear it for miles on a still day — sputtering and bleating, with now and then a blast like a gun as the little engine tried to keep going — crude and in a kind of experimental stage. That was the first gasoline plow in the district, owned by people by the name of Rumpkies.

Neighbors would ride down to see how it worked and go home shaking their heads at the newfangled thing that they saw a man plowing with. But it made sense, anyone could see that; so more and more farmers were buying gasoline tractors to pull their plows.

It was the death knell of the harness business. Who would keep twelve to eighteen horses winter and summer, feed and water them, put up hay, grow oats, do all that extra work, when you could hitch your plow to a tractor, start it, and when the day's work was done, shut it off and let it sit there in the field until the next morning.

I don't believe Jimmy sold a set of harness after 1921. So we went broke.

CHAPTER 46
Homesteading Again

Then, buoyed up by the stories his father had told them about early life in Ontario, Jimmy got the idea of going homesteading. Having put in one session with my parents, I wasn't too keen on the idea. I knew what it meant to take raw land, no matter how good, and break it foot by foot. And ours was prairie land and this was solid bush, and you would have to cut down hundreds of trees before you could set a plow into it. How would that suit him who hated work and everything that went with it.

But, buoyed up by his father's stories, nothing would do but we would try it. He coaxed my brother Clyde to go to Tisdale with him and file on a homestead, and up they went and got one each, about twenty-five miles south of Tisdale. It was solid bush, not so much as an acre clear, just the tall poplars standing like a giant wall as far as the eye could see.

Thank goodness my brother didn't stay. I guess one look at the trees was enough for him. I don't know what he would have done with his wife and five small children in a country where there wasn't enough food to feed a canary.

The eastern side of the homestead ran into muskeg. They didn't know much about muskeg, but we soon learned that it was utterly impossible to do anything with it. It's about the worst kind of land in the world; a few stunted evergreens grow on little hummocks here and there with clumps of slithery earth between them, and if you step into one of them, there is a good chance that you'll never get out alive. There is a sucking feeling and down you go, and there is no possible chance of making it into land.

Later on, when the railroad came through, they lost an entire work train before they learned how to handle it.

Jimmy had borrowed $500 from my uncle (which I had to pay back to him twenty years after when I sold the little farm for exactly that, after Jimmy died). And so one bright morning he loaded a carload of settler's effects for Tisdale, leaving me and the baby with my mother until he could get a roof on the log shack a hundred miles from anywhere.

He got help at Tisdale and managed to get the horses, cows, and hens out to the homestead; then he sent for me and the baby. So up we went. He had come into Tisdale with a hayrack and two horses for us and the household goods piled on it: stoves and beds, upturned tables, and rattling pots and pans.

I didn't feel very poetic, I can tell you, as I sat on a mattress with the baby who dozed and cried and wet her pants. We were packed in like sardines between pillows and old quilts, chairs, tables, a bed and an old table, all rattling and shifting, with the hayrack threatening to turn over entirely when we hit a bad place in the road.

As we got nearer the homestead the road narrowed down to a trail, so Jimmy had to walk ahead with an axe over his shoulder, cutting out the odd poplar tree here and there, to let the hayrack through. All day long the horses plodded on while the mosquitoes and black flies turned the world into a hellish nightmare.

Then Jimmy yelled, "Stop right where you are." I pulled up, not knowing what to expect — Indians or wolves or a new stretch of muskeg. He walked past, his face aglow, and said, "Well, mother, this is where our land starts — right there by that big tamarack."

I caught my first glimpse of our new home through a mist of mosquitoes and tears. I held the baby close to me. It was a rough log cabin that my husband had paid two men to put up the winter before. How desolate it looked with tamarack and poplar trees that stood close around it. The loneliness of it frightened me.

We didn't have much furniture, which was a blessing; we had our old bedroom set, a round table, a couch, three chairs and that's about all.

The floor slanted to one side and had huge knotholes in it where my heels were always getting caught.

Our first night on the homestead was just a forerunner of all the lonely uncomfortable nights that followed. There were mosquitoes, black flies, flying ants, mice running over the bed and our faces, the howling of timber wolves chasing rabbits across the muskegs, and queer unknown noises that we never heard on the prairie.

There was a crude log barn with no roof on it — just the logs thrown across and some straw that had been hauled in and put up. And although we lived there for four years, it never did get a roof on it.

A couple of bachelor neighbors had seen us driving by and walked over to give us a hand with the unloading. I told them to put the baby's cot up first, so they did, and I got her fed and a bit comfortable and she gave a little sigh of happiness and went to sleep with her bottle against her cheek.

Then our bed came next. As there was no board floor in the bedroom end, the bed was set on solid earth; and it sat there for four years without a board floor under it.

Then the men heaved the rest of the furniture in, set up the old cookstove in one corner, pushed the stove pipe through a round hole in the end of the building, started a fire going, and we were on our way.

There were holes cut for a window and a door, but it was months before we got glass for the windows; we used gunny sacks nailed over the opening and we didn't get a door on until October. I used to wake up in the night in terror, thinking a bear had walked in. One never did, but once a cow laid down in the doorway and breathed and sniffed with her head inside the opening, and that scared me stiff too. I guess I just wasn't cut out to be a northern pioneer.

Toward fall, Mrs. Robinson, my good neighbor a mile away, was worried about me; so one day she rounded up her husband and two of his brothers and made them come over and batten up the huge cracks between the logs with mud, and put a door on.

She also sent another neighbor with a buggy to get me and the baby. She said she wouldn't sleep at night worrying for fear we would be found dead some morning, frozen stiff, when Jimmy would be off wandering through the country, since the house wasn't fit for a human being to live in.

I was so glad for this little respite in my scary lot. She cooked nice little meals and was like a mother. I will always remember her and her goodness to me and the baby, when we needed someone to care if we lived or died or froze to death.

Winter came early and by spring everything on the place was dead of starvation, except one horse and a bone-thin cow. We had let the other stock out when the feed ran out, thinking they might hit an old haystack or find something to eat to tide them over; but we found one horse lying on a hill about a mile from home, almost devoured by wolves. We never saw anything of the rest of them, poor things, and if there is a heaven for animals, I hope they found it somewhere beyond the blue.

Only we three humans survived. We lived on oatmeal porridge, dry bread, pancakes and beans — just the bare essentials to keep us alive. Counting calories didn't bother us there; we were all thin as laths.

One of the hardest things was the lack of water in the summer. We had no well and I had to lug it by the pailful from the muskeg about a quarter-of-a-mile from the house. I'd take the baby half way down, tie her to a tree, and then run the rest of the way, get the water, return, untie her, and let her toddle home after me.

I learned to cut wood like a woodsman. We had one of those airtight heaters and it was a corker for using up wood, but it kept the cabin warm as long as we stuffed wood into it. Nights when the fire went out, we crouched under the covers of the bed with only our noses sticking out.

I laugh now as I remember my husband's head on the pillow with his fur cap on, the ear flaps tied under his chin and the peak pulled down over his nose. I wore a wool scarf and often woke up half smothered in its folds.

But it wasn't all misery. I can remember flashes of beauty

and happiness — the sun coming up over the frozen muskeg shining upon the dazzling white snow, the little cleared space of the garden rimmed by evergreen and white birch with the tracks of lynx and deer patterned across its whiteness, and the tiny webbed footprints of the whisky jacks who stayed with us and sang their cheerful songs across the still frozen world.

• • •

I don't believe that Jimmy realized that every foot of ground had to have a tree cut from it before the plow could come in. Although we had the barn, we had no food, no fences, no pens for the chickens or turkeys — they just roamed through the bush and seemed to stay close to the little clearing, as if for security and safety.

It was all right during the summer, but frost came early; the pea vine wilted and the native grass, what there was of it, shriveled at the first frost, and there was nothing for the cows or horses to eat, just nothing. There was no grain for the hens or turkeys; most of them had disappeared anyway. It's likely the wolves got them.

One old hen survived. Along about dusk we would see her heading for home scolding to herself and shaking her feathers, but she laid an egg faithfully every day and I was thankful for that as I had something to feed the baby.

I remember one day hearing her scolding as she rushed home. Instead of going to the barn where she usually laid her egg, she came rushing in the open doorway, got behind the stove and laid her egg there, then ruffled her wings a bit and walked sedately out the door as if to say, "How's that for service."

I am not overly fond of eating, but there was always that constant hunger for decent food. I'd think of my people on the prairie with their cellar full of good cured pork, barrels of it, and the rich cream they always had, and the yellow butter my mother churned every week. I'd think of them going to town on Saturday night in their nice car and meeting the neighbors, and going to Ladies' Aid and to church dressed up like the rest of them. And I'd think of the purple shadows on the flats to the east of us, and the meadow larks singing from every clump of sage and scented brier bush.

I was used to far horizons where you could see for ten miles, but here the trees hemmed you in like a prison; there weren't just a few trees here and there, but solid walls of them on both sides, and crooked stumps that looked like evil men at night creeping toward the house.

For Jimmy was always the wanderer. I'd be left alone for a week or so at a time, not knowing where he was, and afraid of anything that moved or didn't move after dark.

The country was so primitive that the wild beasts were still with us, not yet having learned the fear of man.

Once on a still moonlit night in the winter when I was there with the baby, a pack of timber wolves ran by the house, so close I thought they were coming right inside. They made their kill by the corner of the house, snarling and fighting and bunting into the walls as they tore the rabbit to shreds. A wave of horror swept over me as the awful sounds drilled through my ears. In the morning when I went out, the snow was stained with the bright frozen blood, and as I wiped it off the window, I wept quietly for the little death I couldn't help.

One cold winter night when I was alone, I got the baby fed and into her warm bed and went outside. I was feeling especially lonely and bitter. The moon, reflected on the snow, made it especially beautiful, but I wasn't feeling in a kindly mood. I was mad at everything, including myself.

I leaned against the little pole fence surrounding the cabin, and looked up at the sky and talked to God. "All right," I said, shaking my fist at Him up there in the heavens, "It's your turn now, but some day," I sobbed, "I'll stand on Parliament Hill in Ottawa and they'll honor me."

I don't know who I meant by "they", but last winter, forty years after, I went to Ottawa for a short visit with friends. I had hardly got into my room at the Y.W.C.A. when the phone rang and someone was inviting me to a reception. I gasped out, "How did you know I was here?" and she laughed and said, "Wouldn't you like to know!" Well anyway, the national press women wanted to give me a reception the next night and where do you think it was? On Parliament Hill in a lovely apartment with dozens of women coming up to shake hands with me and to tell me they loved my poetry.

But do you know, all through that lovely evening, little shivers would race over my body, and I could see myself, cold and lonely and leaning on a rail fence at forty below zero in the forest near Tisdale and telling God that some day I would stand on Parliament Hill, and people would be standing in line to meet me.

Knowing God (through the loving kindness of His son when he was on this earth), I know He would smile and perhaps laugh at how He had made my wild prophecy come true.

I might just mention here (since I am boasting), that in 1976 I was made a "woman of the year" by Premier Davies of Ontario, and I humbly thank the committee that so kindly elected me for this great honor.

CHAPTER 47

Neighbors

The second summer we were there, a railway was being built from Wadena to Nipawin, and the right-of-way went right through our quarter section almost cutting it in half. A wide swath of trees was cut out of the solid bush, nearly a quarter-of-a-mile wide, and great piles of trees were burned. How lovely that cleared space looked to me. Often I would walk our little girl up to it, just to see something except trees.

They used scrapers and bulldozers and men with teams to clear the land, and I would talk to the rough, hard-working men, just to hear the sound of my own voice and theirs; and I think most of them were kind of sorry for me; they would pause a few minutes to tell a joke or tell me that their families were on homesteads too, and lonely for them, they hoped.

Toward fall they began to lay the rails, putting down the heavy wooden ties first, then laying the iron rails on them and spiking them down. It looked pretty crude to me and I wondered if real trains could ever travel over it; but they did and I think one of the sweetest sounds I ever heard in my life was the train whistle echoing above the trees, reminding us that there was life somewhere out there beyond the blue. I knew it was a way of escape if I ever needed it.

Our mail used to come to Prince Albert; it was then taken to a post office on the Indian reserve by the name of Chagoness, and then fifteen miles farther on to a homesteader by the name of Wilcox, where it was kept in a box in the corner of the two room log house. We got it there. One time my mother sent me a new violin bow for Christmas and Mrs. Wilcox stuck it behind the flour barrel to keep it safe from the kids, then forgot all about it.

Next summer when she was giving the house a cleanup, she found the bow safe and sound, and the next time we called for the mail we got it. My mother couldn't understand why I didn't write and thank her for her nice gift.

• • •

After that first summer, a few families came in. There was Matt Saborin, a fine hard-working French-Canadian, his wife and a little boy and girl. Matt built a little fourteen-by-twenty foot house and we were glad to have them for neighbors. They would come walking up the little crooked trail to our place and sit and talk for a couple of hours. We hardly ever offered them anything to eat; we didn't have anything to spare, I can tell you.

I remember once my mother had sent me a little box of groceries and in it was a bottle of catsup. We hadn't seen any for two years and nothing ever tasted better. As we had a few bites to spare, I invited them for lunch, and the boy spotted the catsup and started to pour it on his plate, splashing it over everything. I could have killed him, but Jimmy, noticing my rising anger, gave me a "no, no" shake of his head and I managed to keep still. Now, fifty years after, I can laugh about it, but at the time it was sheer tragedy to see my lovely catsup being poured on everything he ate, and to this day I remember it when we get a new bottle of catsup.

Then a nice family by the name of Beatty came in about three miles west of us: a father, mother and five children — two big boys and the three girls. They are still among my best friends. The girls worked their way through the university in Saskatoon, and all three of them married well; they all keep in touch with me. I think they consider me a second mother as both their parents died long ago, and I think of them also, next to my own.

A family of girls moved up from Manitoba, and a few bachelors came along. One was a young fellow, Bob Carlton, a returned soldier from the First World War whose right side had been almost shattered by a gun. He got a little pension, and started a pool room up in the little townsite where there was a tiny station and a store or two. How good it was to see them coming in. Now I knew that if anything happened when Jimmy was away I was within reach of help.

Mr. and Mrs. Howe took up a homestead about three miles east of us; they had two teenage girls, Enid and Blanche, and a little boy by the name of Wardie.

Blanche, the youngest girl, had to walk that long terrible three miles to school every day, so now and then I would invite her to spend a week or so with me when I thought I could afford the extra food.

One late afternoon I was sitting there beside the stove when the door opened quietly, just a crack at a time, and the whitest face I ever saw in my life peeked in. My heart gave a thump; I really thought it was a ghost, but it was Enid; her whole face was frozen stiff and whiter than a dead man's.

After I let out a scream I recognized her and said, "Oh, come in, come in." I helped her unfreeze her poor face, dabbing it with snow, and she never let out a whimper of pain; it must have hurt her terribly, for nothing hurts worse than a face or hand or foot being thawed out. I have seen strong men cry when a hand or foot was being thawed.

After the railroad came through, they brought the mail in on the train, of course. They called the nearest station Barford. It was about a quarter-of-a-mile from us and the mail was thrown off; I became the postmaster for the new office. I kept the mail in a box just like Mrs. Wilcox had, and men would walk for miles on mail day to get news from home. But I don't think Mrs. Wilcox ever forgave us for taking the post office job away from her. We got eleven dollars a month for it, and that was a wonderful help in buying our groceries, although Jimmy took five of it for his tobacco. That always came first.

Then a man by the name of Merton built a little store on the new townsite and we lost our post office and the money. He partitioned off a tiny corner of the store and they were the new postmasters.

As other families started to come, someone decided we

must have a school. And in a short time, there it stood; it was a little one to be sure, but large enough for each of the kids to have a desk. The little teacher was the most popular girl in the district. Indeed, she was about the only real grown-up one, and had every bachelor in the country eating out of her hand. She was a spunky little thing and the mothers liked her, for she gave the kids lots of homework and didn't take any back talk from any of them.

The third summer we had a young missionary come and preach to us now and then in the school. He rode a tall horse and seemed to enjoy his visits with us. We used a pie plate for the collection plate. Once my husband took up the collection and when he finished his round there was only a small five cent piece on the plate, and he announced loudly, "It's a good thing Enid came to church or there wouldn't have been any collection."

CHAPTER 48

A New
Life

One day the conductor of the little train handed me an envelope
with money in it and a letter telling me to come home the next
day; my sister Madge was very sick. The trainmen often
handled messages like that, as there were no phones or any
other way to get in touch with the homesteaders in an emer-
gency.

So the next day when the train came down from Nipawin,
my little girl and I got on and went home. When my brother
met me at Moose Jaw, he told me quietly that she was gone, and
I'll never forget the empty, lonely feeling that swept over me
when I knew I had arrived too late.

She had always been a quiet, gentle girl, none too robust, a
little thing with shiny blue eyes, and a lovely complexion. After
we all left home she was terribly lonely out there on the farm
with only mother and dad. Once she wrote to me, "I am so
lonely, the very walls seem to cry out for you and Arlie." And
indeed it must have been awful in the wintertime, when nothing
moved or seemed to be alive during the long winter months.

I stayed at home for a month and then decided to go back.
I didn't want my marriage to crack up, so that was the only
thing to do.

My mother gave me my train fare, and when the train
pulled into the little station at Barford, there was Jimmy waiting
for me. We walked home and started life again, but it was the
same old story — myself and the little girl holding down the
homestead, Jimmy wandering away for days or weeks on end,

coming home cheerful and never giving any explanation as to
where he had been or what he had been doing.

I guess I was a born sissy; I cried most of the time. I would
start just after breakfast and cry off and on all day long. My
husband must have got sick of the sight of my tears. I cried so
much that never again, no matter what happened, did I ever
shed a tear.

Years after, when my mother died, I couldn't cry, and I
loved her very much. One day dad said to me, "Why don't you
cry?" and I said, "Dad, I can't cry," and he shouted at me,
"Well, you've got to cry at the funeral." My cousin, sitting
there, said quietly, "If she can't cry, she can't cry," and I didn't.
I don't know what the neighbors thought, but there I sat dry-
eyed.

Although still in my mid-thirties, my hair was almost
white, I weighed less than 100 pounds, and was haggard as an
old woman.

I had written a letter to a friend in Briercrest. I don't know
what I said, but she took the letter down and read it to my
father and mother and then announced to them, "We've got to
get her out of there, we just have to, she's going crazy."

They packed up the next week and went to Victoria, rented
a nice furnished house, and sent me a ticket to come out. So one
terribly cold day at the end of November, I left the homestead
forever. I will never forget the almost crazy feeling of happiness
that swept over me when I got on the train. I had made over a
dress of my mother's to fit me, fixed up my little girl the best I
could, and when I sank into the seat of the train, I knew what it
must be like to arrive at the Pearly Gates and watch them open
to let you in.

Dad was at the dock in Victoria to meet me; we got a taxi,
and when we got to their place and the door opened, I knew
again a great rush of joy. I knew I was safe and nothing could
hurt me now.

It was a lovely house with fresh clean white sheets on the
bed, beautiful furniture, and good meals. It was wonderful to
wake up in the night and see the street lights glowing in the
darkness, to feel my little girl near me, to walk on soft carpets
again and to know that we would have a good breakfast in the

morning with toast and marmalade and maybe an orange or grapefruit, with my mother rocking in the big chair, reading a new magazine and muttering to herself as she always did when reading.

How I enjoyed the weeks that followed — just walking the lovely streets without falling over a log, looking over fences at the lovely gardens with flowers in them and green hedges and lawns. The parliament buildings — could Heaven be any lovelier, I wondered. Once, beside a beautiful bed of roses there, I thought I would just smell one of them; as I stooped over to do this I felt a gentle hand on my shoulder and looked up into the faces of a Mountie who was strolling nearby, guarding I suppose.

He said gently to me, "What are you doing?" And I answered him with a rush of joy, "Oh, aren't they beautiful, aren't they beautiful." He smiled and said, "Where are you from?" When I told him that I had just spent four awful years on a bush homestead forty miles west of Prince Albert, he got quite excited and said, "I was stationed in Prince Albert for three years and I know how you feel. Go ahead and smell all you like." We had a good laugh over it.

The Chinese fruit stores killed me to see apples and oranges piled up, bananas, grapes, strawberries, and maybe here and there a big vase of flowers. The Chinese love flowers and often have huge bowls of them among the vegetables just to make a pretty picture, as one nice Chinese boy told me.

Another favorite trip was to the outer wharf to see the great ships there, loading lumber for Britain, or maybe Australia, or Japan. I suppose, being of English descent, the love of the sea is bred in me. The sight of the white ships always warmed my heart, as they were untied and slowly backed up and turned around and then with a blast of the whistle headed for open water and the long voyages across the Pacific Ocean.

My father too, loved to walk down around the docks and watch the boats at the inner wharf backing out carefully. It was such a little place to turn around in. Now and then he would catch his breath and whisper through his teeth, "They're going to hit the dock," and then he would give a sigh of relief when they didn't, and say, as if to himself, "I don't know how they do it. I don't know."

How I loved the streets and houses and people near me. Sometimes I would make a sandwich for myself and my little girl and we'd leave the house around mid-morning and just walk. I didn't have money to squander on streetcar fares. I wanted to walk anyway, to feel a sidewalk under my feet, look over fences at the lovely houses, sit down on a park bench, talk to anyone who might happen to be near me — maybe an elderly man or an old woman who looked friendly and most of the time I found they were prairie people, lonely too, who had come to the coast to escape the long winter on the farm, and like myself, longing for a bit of gossip and friendly talk.

I knew my people would be going back in the spring and suddenly wondered what I would do then. So I went down to Sprott Shaw Business College and arranged to put in two hours a day, on a typing refresher course, which I knew was a good idea.

After we had been there about a month, Jimmy came out. I met him at the dock and he came home with me and stayed a week or so. Then a friend got him a job in a lumber camp up at Yobo. That didn't last long; he was neither a worker nor a lumberman. So one day he appeared at the door again and said he was going back to Barford, I went to the dock to see him off. He looked so nice in his new suit and overcoat as we stood there a few minutes. Then he said, "Well Edna, this is goodbye. I am never coming back. We are breaking up. You have a better chance of looking after the baby than I have. If I look after myself I'll be fine." And then he added quietly, "I know she'll be all right with you." We shook hands, he kissed Joyce, lifted his hat as he had done years before in Briercrest when first I saw him, and walked away toward the boat.

He wrote me a couple of letters and that was the end of it. I never saw him again. Years after, his sister Agnes wrote and told me had had died of cancer. They took his body back to Winchester, Ontario. He is buried there in a little cemetery about five miles from where his grandfather had cut his lovely farm out of the wilderness that was then Ontario.

When I read the letter I said a little prayer for him and added a postscript to it for God to take care of him.

Dorothy Christy, the little girl my mother raised, came with them. She was about eleven at the time, a nice gentle girl. She went to school, and now and then she would take Joyce to the park for a swing, or play on the rocks at Beacon Hill, and make sand pies on the beach. I knew I could trust her.

Then it was coming spring and I knew my parents would be going back to the prairie. The day they left I suddenly felt homeless again. A good friend had said to me one day, "What are you going to do when they go back?" I had answered honestly, "I don't know."

I saw them off at the dock, walked the streets for a couple of hours, then took a streetcar to Cicely's, a friend of mine. I knocked at the door; when she opened it, she took one look at me and said, "Come in."

Her house wasn't very big, but she cleaned out her own bedroom for me. Her husband was a sailor on a deep sea ship and was away most of the time. So she just moved upstairs and put me in her nice comfortable bed off the living room.

After a week I knew this couldn't go on, so I watched the want ads in the paper and came across one that said a lumber office at Chemainus wanted a stenographer. As I had had some experience in a lumber office, I thought I would apply for it.

So up I went, but when the man at the lumber office saw me, he shook his head and said the job had been filled. I knew I looked pale and thin and he didn't want anyone around him that looked like a ghost. So I went out and wondered what I would do. When Jimmy left, I had exactly nine dollars and sixty-five cents in my purse, and I had taken half of it to get up to Chemainus.

But, just about a mile before the bus got to Chemainus, I had looked out the window and seen a lovely little hotel — an English type place — and sitting beside a table on the lawn I had noticed a woman having a cup of tea.

That gave me an idea, so back I walked, out to where she was sitting and told her my story. I made no bones about how I had been refused a job in the mill office, and asked her timidly if she needed help in the hotel. I could wash dishes, make beds, wait on tables.

She answered kindly, "Well no, we don't need anyone right now, but give me your phone number and if we need help I'll phone you."

A few days later Cicely's phone rang and it was Mrs. Collier, the hotel woman, asking me if I could come right up. I answered, "I'll be on the bus tomorrow." I hadn't told her I had a little girl; I was afraid if I did, naturally they wouldn't take me, so now, what was I to do.

But Cicely said, "No, don't tell her. Work a week or so and do a good job, then tell her. I'll look after Joyce. She'll be all right." So with a hundred warnings to her not to play on the road I got the bus and up I went.

I worked like a nailer — made beds, waited on tables, helped with the washing. And then one morning when I was putting the wash on the line and she was helping me, I got up the courage to tell her about Joyce and ask if I could have her with me.

Never to my dying day will I forget her lovely answer, "By all means bring the child up." I couldn't sleep a wink with joy flooding over me. I phoned my friend and she came up with her. We gave her lunch and she took the next bus home and I had my precious kid, safe in bed with me at night. How glad I was — how very glad.

CHAPTER 49

The
Colliers

Mrs. Collier was an easy going boss. In fact, she didn't boss at all. There were two little girls and an older boy, Teddy. He was the hardest one to live with. Now and then he would burst through the swinging dining room doors into the kitchen without any warning; once he almost knocked me over with a full tray. I got mad and told him quietly that if he ever did that again I would tell his father. And as his father was the only person in the world he was afraid of, he kept out of the way during meal times and we never had another run-in.

Mrs. Collier was from Prince Edward Island and Mr. Collier was from England; he was a tall, thin, fine-looking man, with fair curly hair and a nice complexion. He had had a little stroke and had to be careful how he walked, but often in the summer he would take his little girl, Ruth, and my Joyce down to the beach for the afternoon, and it was a great relief to have a bit of peace and quiet without her on my mind.

His mother had been a lady-in-waiting to Queen Victoria. I don't know what on earth brought them to Canada, but in their luggage there was an old solid built trunk filled with old dresses that the queen had discarded. The kids used to go into a little dark baggage room at the end of the hall and dress up in them and parade around upstairs.

One time I thought I would try it also (all the fun hadn't been taken out of me, I suppose), so I picked out a fine stiff black silk dress to try on. It was floor length, tightly gathered at the waist, and the top part was a stiff basque type, boned, with a high neck and fastened with a solid row of silver buttons; there was also a tiny flowered bonnet with bunches of violets on it, and a fluffy veil.

When I put it on, it fitted perfectly. The skirt band was perfect, length the same, and the basque buttoned around me like a glove. I put the tiny hat on, tied the purple ribbons under my chin, and almost scared myself when I looked in the mirror. I was the good Queen Victoria, to a "t".

It was about nine o'clock in the evening and getting dusk. Mr. and Mrs. Collier were sitting in the garden and the kids dared me to go out and show them how I looked. I walked sedately, as I imagined the old queen would, and just before I got to their table, Mr. Collier looked up and turned as white as a sheet, and let out a gasp. He stood up and cried, "You . . . you . . ." and then sank down in his chair and waved me away.

I was told after that he really thought it was the ghost of Queen Victoria, who had come back to earth to scare him. I can tell you I ran for the house and never tried that trick again.

I stayed there about a year, and I must say that never was the hired help treated better. I have thanked them a hundred times in my heart for being so kind and nice to me.

Then, one day I received a letter from Jimmy that had been sent to Briercrest and forwarded to me. He was living in his old home on a farm near Winchester and he wanted to know if I would come back East and we'd try to make a go of it again.

I thought it over and decided to give it a try. Surely, I told myself, he would work there on the old farm. So I told my boss that I was leaving. He put his hand on my shoulder, and in his gentle way, thanked me for staying with them for so long.

I bought myself a nice new outfit and a little blue sailor coat and cap for Joyce. He didn't send me any money for my fare, but told me to stop off at Briercrest, visit my people, and then come on. When I got to Briercrest, there was another letter waiting for me from him, telling me to stay where I was, that his plans had changed. His sister told me years after that he had no intention of having me come East; he just wanted to get me away from the coast. I cannot imagine why.

And there I was again, home and broke. My parents had

sold the farm to my brother Clyde in 1929, and taken a tiny house in town; I knew I couldn't stay with them. And although the drought had started and crops were next to nothing, Clyde said to me, "Come on out to the farm for the winter, and we'll all starve together."

CHAPTER 50

The Farm
Again

I gathered up my things, put them in a suitcase and Clyde drove us out to the farm in his old battered Ford. So I was back where I started, only feeling a bit of a stranger in the rooms that looked so different with their furniture in them, and not the nice comfortable things my mother had.

His wife, Mary, said, "We've fixed up the little east room for you and Joyce. I hope you will feel at home, and remember you are just as welcome here as any of the rest of us."

So up I went, back in the little room where I had slept years ago. Mary had put an old feather tick on it, clean flannelette sheets and a nice white spread, with a little old pot under the bed, just where it used to sit. It seemed to be the last straw making me feel at home. And there was a stove pipe running through the room into the brick chimney giving a bit of heat, even on the coldest days.

The window faced east, down across the flats with their purple shadows; there was the smell of sage, and brier, and that peculiar prairie smell that you never forget — maybe from something coming up from the earth that, even to this day, is drying out from the centuries of time that it lay beneath salt water.

There were nine of us. Mary and Clyde and their five children, Joyce and me. Clyde had run the local elevator before he took over the farm, but that fall, 1929, there wasn't a bushel of wheat coming in as the drought started and the elevator was practically closed. So Clyde got the job of caretaker and received thirty-five dollars a month for it, and that is precisely what we lived on that winter. Now and then I would sell a poem and buy a bag of flour or ten pounds of sugar, or some little treat such as a pail of jam or a can of syrup.

During the winter (especially with a blizzard on), it got pretty tough. Somtimes for a week at a time, the older kids couldn't go to school. They just couldn't face a blizzard in an open buggy, their only mode of travel except to walk, and that was too hard, especially for the little ones.

Joyce and their youngest boy, Bryon, never went. We were afraid they would freeze, so I taught them at home for a couple of hours each day. When they went to school to try the Easter exams for grade two, they both passed with flying colors.

Now and then, when the weather was too bad for anyone to go, it got pretty hectic, with six kids whooping and hollering and fighting. But with it all, my good sister-in-law and I never had a mean word between us. She was a saint and still is — pretty, and the best Christian I ever met in this world, loving and kind. I don't believe she ever had a mean thought in her head. So we kept the peace and I still love her very much.

Although there wasn't much feed for the horses, Clyde managed to keep them alive that first winter. He let them out early in the spring, hoping they would find enough to keep them going until the grass grew.

Both of my brothers got the land seeded in the spring of 1930, in spite of the drifting soil and no rain. They hoped against hope that some kindly power on high would send a few showers and get the seed started. But no showers came. Then the wells began to dry, first one, then another, and the little bit of water in the ponds except in the one deep well that only gave enough to keep the house going, if you were careful.

I'll never forget the awful day my brothers decided they would have to shoot the horses; there were twenty-seven of them, standing in the yard with their heads down, slowly dying of thirst. In a community pasture a few miles from us, 118 horses died of thirst, their tongues sticking out, swollen and blistered. Clyde said, "I'll never let mine die of thirst. I couldn't stand it."

So one terrible morning, they rounded all their horses up,

led them down to the far corner of the farm on the flats, and shot them one by one. When Clyde pulled the gun on his favorite one, a beautiful saddle horse called Fred, the horse let out a little whinny, as a person would shake hands with a special friend. Clyde pulled the trigger and got him square in the center of his forehead, and he never knew what hit him.

I never saw grown men cry like my brothers did that day. Clyde just lay on his bed all that fearful Sunday and cried until he couldn't see out of his eyes. And I know Bruce did the same.

CHAPTER 51

The
Drought

It was in 1929 that the drought started, and for nine terrible years there were no crops in Saskatchewan, that is, in the southern part. The land was desolate — gray ashy wastes that once were fields, white alkali flats that once were sparkling little lakes. In our gardens there weren't even any weeds — just the driven soil resting for a few days until another wind would come up and drive it in another direction.

Drought never comes alone; it travels with ill-starred company — grasshoppers and queer flies that we never saw before. A new kind came that spring (as if we didn't have enough). It had the head of a fly and the body of a mosquito, and when it bit horses they staggered like drunken men, their throats swelled up and they were dead in a few hours.

The army worms came too in massed formation, in uniforms of bottle green. We watched them come up the sidewalk of the little village, swarming the width of it like filthy water, flowing toward the little gardens where some faithful soul had watered. They are blind and never turn out of their way for anything.

One morning I heard a piercing scream and ran out. It seemed that all the women were out waving their aprons and wringing their hands. It was the army worms coming like a curse, relentlessly, inevitably. The road was covered with them; the sidewalks and fences were alive.

We tried to head them off. We dug trenches and filled them with oil and set fire to them, killed them with hoes and shovels and sticks. They might just as well have tried to stem the tide of the Pacific.

One woman had watered her beans, guarded them and was hungry for them, but the army worms swarmed over them. In a few minutes there were no beans left and she went into the house and cried helplessly into her apron.

The worms fed on Russian thistle too, about the only thing left in the country, and the cattle ate the thistles and died from the poison that had been set out for the worms.

Sudden freak storms came too, as if the elements fought some mighty war in the air. The sky would be a black-blue. You would think a million tons of water would be held in the inky depths, but it was only dust and wind, and maybe a few scattered drops of rain — cyclone air that made it hard to breathe, as your heart pounded against your ribs in sickening thuds.

CHAPTER 52

The Turning
Point

One evening the phone rang. Clyde answered it, then turned and said to me, "A woman in Moose Jaw wants to talk to you." Wondering who it could be, as I didn't know three people in the city, I went to the phone and said, "Hello."

She said her name was Mrs. Peacock, president of the Women's Canadian Club, and would I come in and speak at their next meeting. I gasped out, "Oh, I just couldn't do that, I never spoke at a meeting in my life. I wouldn't know what to talk about," and she said, "Oh, you mustn't be afraid of us. We all love your poetry, and you can just get up a little talk and we'll love it." Again I hestiated and she added, "I'll give you twenty-five dollars if you will come." At that time I would have let them cut a leg off me for twenty-five dollars and I said, "I'll come."

I turned to Clyde and told him what she had said and I added, "I don't know what to say, or how to say it, or how to keep from dropping dead on the platform." And Clyde answered me, "Sure you can. You just go up on the platform and start talking; tell them the little stories you tell us, and finish with a poem — five or six of them will take about a half-hour. Sure you can." He added, "I'll rig the old car up and take you in. You'll be all right."

So up we went, plowing through drifted soil, huge banks of it right in the middle of the road, and snow banks. Sometimes the old car would slow down and dig its toes in like a horse, and then pull out of it, and before I knew it, there we were right in front of the Grant Hall Hotel. How big and imposing it looked compared to the little store and houses in our village.

Clyde said, "You go in. I'll park the car and come and be with you. Are you sure you've got your speech?"

When I got inside, Mrs. Peacock was waiting for me in the lobby. She came up, shook hands, smiled and said, "My, you are such a little person." She didn't know how little I felt, but as we went up to the hall on the second floor, quite a few spoke and smiled. Then an old friend, Isabel Shaw, leaned over when she went by and whispered, "I am praying for you Edna dear. You'll be all right."

When I was introduced to the ladies, they gave me a nice reception. I had picked out a half-dozen poems, told how they came to be written like a story, then quoted the poems. After I got started, most of my nervousness went away. They laughed and clapped. I could see my brother at the back of the room, his facing shining with happiness that I was doing well. But I can tell you I heaved a lovely sigh of relief when it was over, and I knew I had done all right.

How were we to know that this meeting was the turning point of my whole life, that from then on, nothing would ever be the same again for me; from that little gathering, a thousand roads would open up for me, a thousand meetings; for the next ten years I would travel thousands of miles, meet thousands of people, stand on a thousand platforms, and wind up fifty years after with clubs and churches and institutes still calling me from across the continent to come and speak to them.

CHAPTER 53

More Speaking
Engagements

One day, toward the end of winter, I thought I would go into town for the weekend; it would be a little break for both Mary and myself. So early next morning I bundled Joyce up and we rode into town with Clyde when he went to work. I could sleep on the couch at my mother's and I knew I could find a bed for Joyce with a good neighbor.

After a little tour of the town, meeting a few friends and having a little gossip, we had supper. Dad went to bed early and maw and I were sitting talking when we heard a knock at the door. She said, "I wonder who that could be at this hour of the night (it was about nine p.m.). So she went to the door and a huge man stood there in a fur coat.

He told us he was Gordon Ross, the M.P. for Moose Jaw. So we invited him in. We talked a little while and then he said to me, "How would you like to come into Moose Jaw and work for me in the office? We are putting on a campaign and I think you would be a great help; and then, if I am re-elected in the fall, I will take you to Ottawa with me, and I think it would work out fine for us all. I need someone down there who knows what I am talking about, and you might help me write my speeches."

My heart nearly stopped beating for a minute, and I gasped, "I would love it." Then he got up, and as he started up the street, walking up the snowy sidewalk in his old black fur coat, the angel Gabriel in all his glory couldn't have looked any more beautiful to me than he did.

It didn't take me long to gather up my clothes, pack a suitcase and get to Moose Jaw. I found a room with a friend and started work the next week. My mother said, "Leave Joyce with me. We'll take care of her and she can go to school here too. It will do her good."

How wonderful it was to be back in an office, taking letters, writing or helping with speeches, feeling useful and part of the world again. Just going out to lunch with a few of the women from the office, talking and laughing and being part of the busy world I loved, was sheer heaven.

But alas, it was short lived. Gordon was defeated in the fall election and my job was gone. So back I went to Briercrest, wondering what the good Lord had in store for me now.

A few days after this a letter came from the C.P.R. office in Montreal, and in it was a pass to Victoria. How or why, or who sent it, I will never know, but there it was. Some good angel must have told them that I would like to go back to the coast. So back we went, Joyce and me, sitting up all the way. Even with a pass I didn't think I could afford a berth; I was on my own again and canny with money.

When we got off the boat, we walked a few blocks. I thought, "I'll get a room somewhere and start again from scratch." We turned a few corners when I saw a notice on the door of a shabby old house, "Room to Rent." So I went up and knocked at the door. A woman opened it and when I inquired about the room, she opened a door from the dingy hall and said, "Well, there it is." I looked in; it was clean, there was a little airtight heater, a bed, a small table with a few dishes on it, and a little pile of driftwood behind the stove, and I said, "I'll take it," and we just moved in.

I went down the street a bit, found a little corner store, bought a loaf of bread, a quart of milk, butter, jam and a dozen eggs. We had our little supper and I put Joyce to bed, warm and safe again from the terrors by night. And in some queer way that little room was homelike, with other people upstairs, a bit of laughter, the door in the hall opening and shutting. I wouldn't be alone anyway, and that was a great comfort. And I seemed to know, even there in that cheap rooming house, that

God hadn't forgotten us, and as the Bible said, was keeping watch over His own.

We found a nice school a few blocks away and Joyce got started to school. And so our little routine started all over again. I had saved a bit of money by then and wasn't unduly worried. After school and on weekends, we would walk to the beach about a half-mile away. She would play in the sand while I wrote my poetry; we would build a little fire and have a lunch, gather small bits of driftwood for our little stove and drag it home on a little borrowed cart. It doesn't sound very glamorous, but we were easily satisfied and best of all, safe and warm. That was the main object in life as far as I was concerned.

One day there came a gentle tap at my door. I opened it and a nice smiling woman said, "I'm Mrs. Wilson. My husband is the minister of the United Church here. We are from Moose Jaw. I had a letter from a friend there telling me that you spoke at the Canadian Club and that you were wonderful."

I gasped out, "Sit down. I'm not wonderful at all." I said, "I was scared stiff all the time I was on the platform." And she laughed, "Well, I've come to ask you to speak to our Canadian Club here. Will you? I'll give you fifty dollars, please come." Fifty dollars, why that would take us through the winter. "Oh, do you think I am good enough for Victoria?" And she laughed and said, "I think you are."

The fateful day arrived. I got a friend to come with me and keep Joyce quiet while I was on the platform. As we walked up the sidewalk toward the Empress Hotel, I said to her, "My, there's an awful lot of cars here, isn't there?" She smiled and said, "Yes." Little did I know what faced me there. It was a combined meeting of the Canadian Club and the Music Club of Victoria. When we went in, the place was packed with women. Someone yelled, "There she is," and someone made a dive for me and hauled me into a circle of a dozen women, all buzzing and excited. One of them said, "My, you are so little to handle such a big meeting. Will you be all right?"

Shivering inside I said, "Sure," and we went in. The huge ballroom was packed to the very last inch. We went up on the platform, took our seats, and the meeting got underway with me looking down at 500 faces, smiling, and I knew, wishing me well.

When the president, Mrs. Scurrah, introduced me and I got up, a queer thing happened. I saw (I swear), a shadowy figure cross the back of the room. She was little and bent with a black shawl over her head. She was smiling at me and to this day I swear it was the ghost of some Irish ancestor telling me I was going to be all right.

I cannot remember how I started or what I said, but a little ripple of laughter swept over the hall, and from that minute I knew I had them. Stiff old dowagers, mothers, younger women, they all laughed in the right places. Egged on by their approval, I forgot all my shyness and the meeting was what one woman said, "a howling success".

After the meeting we had tea. Someone handed me a cup and I never got one sip of it, or a bite to eat. They stood in line to shake hands, and I got more invitations to come to tea than I could fill in five years. I remember Emily Carr, the artist, with her dog. She made me shake hands with him, and everyone thought it was nice.

They gave me a huge sheaf of flowers, the first bouquet I had ever received in my life. The next day I sent it by express to my mother in Briercrest, and she took it to the Ladies' Aid and they all admired it — the one and only bouquet that they probably had ever seen. My mother said it stayed fresh for three good weeks, and everyone in the village came to see it; even the kids knocked at the door and asked shyly if they could see Edna's flowers.

It happened that Mrs. Scurrah, the president of the club, and her husband had a high class ladies ready-to-wear store. She came to see me next day and ask me if I would like to come and work part time in their office. For five years I worked there mornings, and so was home when my little girl got home from school. It was an ideal arrangement, and Mrs. Scurrah was the one person in the world that I needed.

She was the regional president of every Canadian Club in British Columbia; and as I learned later, for the whole of Canada. One day she asked me if I would go up to Port Alberni and speak to the club there, and I said, "Sure." That also proved a success, and from then on she sent me out to every club in B.C. Then the head office in Ottawa wrote and asked me if I would make a trip across Canada, and that was the beginning. For five solid years I crossed and recrossed Canada, into just about every hole and corner of the Dominion from Halifax to Prince Rupert. It was fantastic.

We had found a nice apartment. The upstairs of a relative had been fixed up nice and cozy, and I knew if I was late or away, Mrs. Taylor would get Joyce in and give her supper and see that she was in bed on time. It was a comfort to me, as they were elderly and seldom went out at night and they were kind and good to us all while we stayed with them.

CHAPTER 54

Nellie McClung

My friendship with Nellie McClung was one of the nicest things that ever happened to me, and although we were a generation apart as to age, we had the same prairie memories, the same general knowledge of work and herding of cattle when young, and were both Jacks-of-all-trades around the farm; we both experienced coming home in the gentle twilight of a summer day, herding our small flocks of cattle into corrals to be milked, where smudge fires burned and the sun went down behind the rim of the world.

I had met her only once when I was speaking to the Authors Club in Calgary. She was nice and friendly, and then when Mr. McClung retired and they moved to Victoria, as soon as they got settled in an apartment, she drove downtown to where I worked, came in and asked for me. When I came downstairs from the office where I worked, she shook hands warmly and invited me to come over the next Sunday. That started a friendship that never wavered or dimmed until the sod was laid over her.

In the spring they bought a little farm of five acres about five miles out toward Gordon Head, and they named it Lantern Lane and it became a lovely second home for me and my little girl. Sunday morning I would see Mr. McClung waiting at the bottom of the church steps, and with a "Come on, Edna," he would take my arm and lead us to their big car waiting at the curb with her in it, telling me to get in; away we would go to a nice hearty lunch, an afternoon of talk and visiting, then supper and home. I always had a glow in my heart at her friendliness to a small struggling person just getting a toehold in the writing world of which I was so ignorant.

When my first little twenty-five cent books came out, she bought them by the dozen, passed them around to her friends telling them to get them instead of Christmas cards as they said so much more and I needed the money.

Some of my loveliest memories are there in their lovely place, with peaches growing up against the house for warmth, cherry trees in rows with their white blossoms in the spring, and then the red fruit in the fall that they could hardly sell because the prairie market was so far away and the boat trip from Victoria to Vancouver added too much to the shipping costs.

Mr. McClung was a great worker; he would be up early and hoeing and working around the place or in his garden; he enjoyed every minute of it. Then there would be supper in the kitchen, like any old farm family with a little wood fire burning in a small cookstove with plenty of good honest food on the table and "himself" on a rocking chair; how wholesome it was, how good. By nine o'clock he would start upstairs to his bed, stopping halfway to say goodnight, and the rest of us would read or type or play the piano for a little while longer, then go to bed too; quiet would settle down around us like a warm blanket on a winter night.

The last time I saw her she was very sick. I had been speaking here and there in Northern British Columbia and Alberta and doing a story for *Maclean's* magazine. After I got this finished, I decided to make a side trip to the coast in order to see her and really know how her health was.

When I got off the boat in Victoria, Mr. McClung was there at the dock to meet me. After we got in the car I said, "Why didn't she come to meet me too?" He answered, "Oh, Edna, she isn't very well." When I got into the house, Helen, their housekeeper, said quietly, "She's in bed." When I saw her I knew she was worse than I had been led to believe.

I got a chair and sat down beside her, patting the covers and smiling with joy to see her again. After we talked a while she said, "Edna, if I have a heart attack, you go out of the room.

Helen knows what to do." And then I realized that it was serious.

I stayed a few days with them. While I was there I had a meeting of the Canadian Club in the Empress. When I got back to Lantern Lane I started to make a "fun report" to her of the meeting; she started to laugh and then said, "Oh, Edna, don't tell me any more; I might get another attack." So I just sat there quietly, patting her hand and telling her about my trip. That was the last time I saw the best friend I ever had in my life, and the most loved, outside of my mother.

When she went in September, 1951, her son, Mark, sent me a telegram that she was gone; that night I cried myself to sleep and asked God to be sure and take good care of her and introduce her to my mother.

CHAPTER 55

My
Plan

On my last trip across Canada doing the cities for the Canadian Clubs, 1935 I think it was, I stopped over in Montreal for a couple of days and stayed at the old Windsor Hotel, a homey place where older people often put in the winter months in peace and comfort. And it wasn't too expensive. I wanted to see my friend Murray Gibbons of the C.P.R. publicity department and put a proposition to him. So the next day I phoned and he said I could come over and talk to him. Sitting across the desk from him I told my plan; I wanted to go here and there in the prairie provinces too, speaking wherever and whenever I got a chance and I couldn't pay train fare as they couldn't pay me much for a meeting. But if I had a railway pass, I thought I could go into just about every little place and speak to them about my poetry, tell stories, and maybe cheer them up.

"Look," I said, pointing to a huge map of Canada under a glass on his big desk, "Here they are: Regina, Assiniboia, Limerick, Eastend, Kincaid, Shaunavon, Bracken." I hardly missed a place in all the little lines that branched out from Moose Jaw, the divisional point. "From there to Portal, Coderre, Shamrock, Esterhazy. . . ."

So he smiled and wrote a little note on C.P.R. stationery telling every C.P.R. ticket agent to give me whatever I asked for. The ticket agent in Moose Jaw said, "How the hell did you get the C.P.R. to give you such a pass?" I laughed and said, "Well, you know mister, even big companies have hearts in them," and he slapped the counter and gave me a sheaf of tickets.

At that time the drought was at its worst with not a living bit of green in all the countryside, no money coming in, no business, no nothing.

Once, in the awful drought years, in a small place where I was to speak, the women of the village and country gave me a lovely lunch. After we finished I thanked them and said, "Now, may I ask you a question?" And they said, "Go ahead." "How, if you are all starving, can you put up such a lovely lunch?" And one woman laughed and said, "Well, you know, everyone brought something. I was saving a jar of pickles for Christmas, but I brought it along." Another woman said, "My sister sent me a dollar so I could have a treat, and I bought the cheese." Another one made a cake; her hens hadn't all died and she had eggs. And one had just killed their last pig and she had lard and made two pies.

There was no self pity; they were cheerful and lovely.

"Now the dresses," I said. "You are all dressed lovely, and I know it must be nearly five years since you could afford a new dress." And one nudged her friend and said, "Go ahead, Em, where did your dress come from?" She said, "My sister in Ontario sent it to me for Christmas." Another one in a lovely blue viole said, "My sister washed this dress and it shrunk and wouldn't go around her, so I got it." All stories were told with laughter, and honest-to-goodness spunk.

I left the town ashamed for ever being sorry for myself, when these valiant women, as brave as any soldier on any battlefield, were smiling through; and if they are alive today I would like to say, "God bless you everyone."

• • •

Thousands of people had hay fever from the blowing dust, their faces swollen or broken out with tiny sores; but they blew their noses in unison in duets and choruses and laughed about it. That was their salvation — they laughed about it — bless their brave hearts.

Perhaps they cried at home, I know they did, cried over

shabby children, poor food, and no gardens. But they didn't cry when they were out. They donned the shining armor of the crusaders and comforted each other and assured themselves that next year it would be better.

There were hundreds of children who did not know what rain was. My brother's little girl, Betty, who was five, came running into the house one day screaming in terror; when her mother asked her what had frightened her, she said, "Water is coming out of the sky."

And so I went to them, speaking in churches, little bare halls; I think maybe I did some good. They said I did anyway, and as long as I live I will remember their upturned faces, listening with now and then a tear running unheeded down a thin cheek and then a hasty look for a handkerchief to wipe it off.

You can't beat people like that. And now, over forty years after, many of them are still there, getting old I know, but laughing and telling you how thin they got and how awful it was.

Now, a lot of these farms have their sons on the same land, and they are prosperous and happy with nice new houses, big cars and as one man said, "I wouldn't call the king me uncle!"

Up and down the country little groups in the villages and countryside wanted to hear me; as requests came in, I would line them up in order to shorten the train trips.

Then I went to Alberta, where every prairie club seemed to want to hear my little talk. From Edmonton I rode the railway to Dawson Creek, the end of steel, speaking at nearly every small town along the right-of-way — Grande Prairie, Red Deer, Spirit River, and dozens of small villages I never heard of. But there was always a happy bunch of women with shining faces, and after we always had a nice lunch. It seems that no matter where you go, there are always women who make nice cakes with pink icing on them. It's a wonder I didn't weigh a ton, but I guess that, in between times, I ran or worked it off.

I remember one little place; a teacher from the country had brought her whole school to the concert in a sleigh pulled by a team of horses and kept warm with lots of blankets. How nice the kids were as she shepherded them up to the platform to meet me. She had told them that they must all say something nice when they were introduced, and to this day I can only remember two of them. One little girl said, "I loved your sermon," and a little boy muttered crossly, "You talked too long."

CHAPTER 56

England

It's a hard thing to raise a child without a home. As I look back on it now, I marvel that my daughter was so unspoiled over it; sometimes in Victoria, or Briercrest, Saskatchewan, wherever it was convenient for me and all right for her, I kept her.

But a few months after my return to Victoria, I thought I had better get her settled for the next few years, so back we went to Saskatchewan. I had heard of a fine United church boarding house for girls in Assiniboia, so we tried that. But the matron was overbearing and rather cross, and Joyce was getting so subdued and depressed that I knew I had to get her out of there. So I applied and got her into Luther College in Regina. There she was with girls of her own "kind", full of fun and laughter, and she tells me now that the two years there were the happiest of her life.

Taking up lecturing again, I would make a point of stopping off in Regina whenever I could; I could see the happy change in her and she made her grades with happiness and ease.

• • •

One day while visiting my mother in Briercrest, resting from the lecturing, dad went down for the mail and threw a letter on the table for me. I looked at the thin envelope and said, "Who could be writing me from B.C.?" When I opened the letter, I found it was from a lawyer telling me that an old man had died and left me $2000.

I couldn't believe my eyes. I had never heard of him, let alone seen him, but the letter said that the man had loved my poetry and from the poems he sensed that I was hard up. So in his will this kindly man had left me the money. I never slept for three nights hand running. Then I said to my mother, "Do you know what I am going to do? I am going to take a trip to the Old Country. I've wanted to go all my life and I might never have enough ahead to do it and before it's all spent I am going."

My mother, in her usual enthusiastic way, said, "Go ahead. I'll never see it, but I'll be glad to hear all about it from you." And so in less time than it takes to tell it, I was on my way. I left by train for New York, got a boat from there (I forget its name), bought an extra railway ticket in Toronto for the British Isles for fifty dollars that was good for a month. You could travel day and night if you wanted to without costing you an extra cent. Of course you paid your own hotel bills and meals.

When we got to Liverpool I took the train to Newcastle, where our adopted sister lived, visited her for a week and then went north, stopping whenever the notion took me. I would find a Y.W.C.A. or a cheap little hotel and it was the most wonderful trip of my life, just browsing, and never having an unpleasant incident in all the month long. I would stop a nice looking woman on the street and ask directions to where I wanted to go, and they were all so nice. They recognized my Canadian accent and always had a smile, or asked if I knew a relative of theirs who had emigrated to Canada twenty or forty years before.

After my visit with Dorothy, I continued north, and it seemed to me that after we crossed the border into Scotland, the very air changed. There was a new odor in the air; it might have been the heather or a different kind of grass, or something in the rocky soil that gave off a smell or perfume that told you you were in a different country. Maybe that was what made the early Scotch so warlike, as clans battled each other for little valleys and pasture land for their sheep. Anyway it was different.

I got to Dundee late one night dog tired, and went to the Y.W.C.A. You know, in the Old Country if you pay for a bed, you always get breakfast thrown in, so I said to the woman at the desk, "I'm awfully tired, so I'll just sleep in and not bother with breakfast. I'll get it in a restaurant when I decide to get up." And she said, "I'll bring it up to you." Then she laughed and handed me my key.

At nine o'clock the next morning I heard a knock at my door. I called "Come in," and there she was with a huge tray fairly loaded down with food: a big bowl of porridge, a plate of toast, marmalade, butter and a huge blue pot of tea. I gasped out, "You're crazy," but she set it on a little table near me, then sat down on a chair and talked a blue streak all while I had that most delicious breakfast. And as long as I live I will see her there, asking about Canada and if I thought she would like it.

From Dundee I went north to Aberdeen, spent two days wandering around that ancient city, down little narrow streets and the broad front streets; I peeked in windows and wandered through the shops, as they call them there. Everywhere I went people smiled at me or spoke and stopped to have a little chat, likely seeing in my different way of dressing that I was some crazy old woman looking for the gold at the end of the rainbow.

Ireland came next. I forget where I got the boat for Ireland. I know I got a berth and slept like a top. And then it was morning and by good luck I got a seat on a big tourist bus that was just starting out from Dublin, following the coastline south, past Wexford where the Kennedys came from, past Cork, up over the hills but still following the coast, past Bangor and Derry where the battered Canadian ships steamed triumphantly in during the war after the terrible crossing of the Atlantic where the U-boats were making every trip a nightmare. How sweet Lough Foule must have seemed to them as they came into its sheltering arms, how good the docks of Derry as they tied their brave ships in the quiet lea of the sheds.

And how lovely it was then with curlews calling from every tree and hedge, and shamrocks carpeting the hillsides past little whitewashed cottages that looked exactly like the pictures. How small they were. I wondered how a family could grow up in them; maybe they had a little attic or a lean-to where they could stack the kids at night.

I often wondered if I might catch a glimpse of someone playing a golden harp, or pluck a few bitter leaves of the shamrock and hear the curlews calling across the green meadows beside the Shannon, or maybe hear someone singing "Danny Boy" across the fields.

I left the coach at Limerick, stayed a night there, and then took a local bus back to the little village of Glin beside the Shannon, where my mother's family came from 140 years before. There I found an old stone inn with walls three feet thick; I got a huge cold bedroom with a giant-sized bed with feather ticks over and under, and a little latticed window that looked like a picture in a tourist folder; I put on my good flannelette nightgown and wool bed socks and sank into its folds and was asleep in five minutes.

The next morning I went hunting relatives and found them a little way out in the country. I knocked, and when they opened the door I told them who I was, that my mother was an O'Donohue from Glin and I would like to visit for a while. They opened the door, told me to come in, and we had the grandest talk. "Sure," said the old man, "Me father's brother went to Canada. I remember them talking about it, and how they missed him to this very day." The oldest son was there, Thomas O'Donohue; his face had a familiar look and I knew I had struck the right people.

Then Thomas showed me how he made their living, by cutting peat from the bog near by — little oblong pieces that he piled up in a stack so the wind could get through and dry it out. Then he sold it to the villages around for fuel. There is no lovelier smell on earth than a peat fire smoldering and sending out tiny sparks of light across a room.

Then we had tea with the best bread I have ever tasted in my life. The loaf was a huge round one and I asked her how she baked it without an oven. She said, "Father, get the pot," and father went out to a little shed and brought in a huge iron pot with three little feet on it and a handle. She showed me how she hung it on a little rod over the fireplace, got the fire down to glowing coals and there it was baked to perfection. I could hardly believe it. So we had our tea and a nice visit. Thomas, the son, writes to me now and then and even sent me some lovely poetry that he wrote.

After seeing Ireland I crossed back to England, got a bus

and went to London, and could hardly believe I was there. It looked exactly like the hundreds of pictures I had seen of it — Trafalgar Square, the Tower, the huge sprawling Parliament buildings, the Thames flowing quietly by as it has done since the beginning of time itself.

I walked up the center aisle of Westminster Abbey as if I had known it all my life. I gazed in wonder at the coronation chair in the middle of the platform, with the flat gray stone under the seat; they claim the stone was the one Jacob slept on and had his dream of angels coming down from heaven to bless him and his poor wandering tribe, seeking rest for the tired soles of their feet.

How traditional I found the English, how careful of it. They cherish the past and as I thought then, how wonderful it is; it's really like a solid rock foundation under a house that is there, secure even if the house falls or governments change and generations pass. There it is — something to build on again as old as the earth.

I sat in a little park across from Buckingham Palace and saw people peeking through the bars of the fence, saying nothing, just looking and being glad to be there, hoping to catch the glimpse of a face in an upper window, or maybe see a door opening and someone coming out to get into a car and drive away. I was suddenly glad that I belonged to it: London, the streets and parks, shops and sidewalks, and even the people who often smiled at me as I passed by.

I met some Canadian friends and together we went out to Windsor Castle and ate our lunch in the park, a good distance from the castle of course, but it was nice to look up from eating a sandwich and see the gray towers and turrets. And it seemed natural, somehow, to be there.

After lunch I strolled around by myself. At the front door a guard was standing, stiff as a poker. I went up to him and said, "I am from Canada and I would love to have a little piece of ivy from the hedge. Do you think anyone would mind?" He never batted an eye or moved a muscle but muttered through his lips, "Go around the corner and nip off a little piece, I shan't be looking." So I did as I was told and now I have a little hanging pot of English ivy from Windsor Castle. My daughter bought me a little copper pail and it hangs before the fireplace in the den, and I am so glad I have something from the Old Land to cheer me up when the news gets bad.

I saw Canterbury, where tradition says the early Christian refugees came after the crucifixion. It is claimed there, that Joseph, the uncle of Jesus, whose tomb He was laid in, brought a shipload of them for safety when they were being persecuted by the Romans.

There is a huge bush nearby; tradition also says that Joseph brought the crown of thorns that Jesus wore and planted it there, and there it is to this day, its great prickly thorns sharp as needles. Thousands believe it, and who can say it isn't true.

The trip home was uneventful. I think I was too tired to enjoy anymore, but the sight of my mother's face and a good supper was enough for me to get my feet on solid ground again and get a new start at whatever came up.

CHAPTER 57

The Munitions Plant

After Joyce finished her grade twelve, we moved to Toronto and she started in on her nurse's course in the Women's College Hospital, and I went to stay once again with my good friend Mrs. Dawkins for a rest.

One night there was a notice in the paper that they needed munition workers. The war was getting worse every day and every hour, and poor old England was being bombed nearly out of existence. So out I went to Ajax to the munition plant and got a job. I worked there for about nine months and wrote a story that appeared in *Maclean's* magazine called, "We Are The Workers." I received many letters from far and near and then forgot about it.

If you worked at the plant, you would rise up when it was still night, like the woman in the Bible, and grope along the half dark street to the car line. You would think you were the only person in the world who was up, but down the dark street you would see another figure moving in the darkness, someone like yourself with her lunch in a greasy bag, picking her way among the puddles or snow, going to work. Another and another would loom up, and by the time you reached the car line, they were coming from every direction — old and young, gay and sober, all finding in the munition work a new way of life.

At the end of the car line, we were met by buses and taken to the plant. We lined up two abreast and waited our turn. Up the buses came and we were quickly loaded and driven off into the darkness, the red lights bobbing down the road like crimson flares to light the way for all to follow them.

There were hundreds and hundreds of us, and deep down in our hearts, we were happy and dimly satisfied that we were part of that gigantic struggle that embraced all mankind in its deadly grip.

At the entrance of the plant stood an armed guard (remember, this was a powder plant.) We had to show our pass and be waved in. Now we were in the danger zone. It scared us a bit at first; we had visions of being hurled through space in the wake of an explosion, but we soon forgot it and handled our dangerous stuff with all the nonchalance of a country woman setting a batch of bread.

There was a huge change house where we took off our street clothes right down to the last two garments, our shirt and pants, where we were inspected by two women sitting beside the door. We would go through and pass into the clean area where no bobby pins were allowed, no cigarettes or metal clasps because of the explosive danger where the very air was charged with explosives and the tiniest spark might set the whole place on fire.

Once past the barrier, we were given clean white uniforms, white caps, and wooden shoes with no nails in them — just wooden pegs and uppers of hand-sewn elk.

Going through another door, we entered a long "clean-way" or hall. These were painted a gleaming white and had hardwood floors and hundreds of lights. They looked for all the world like the deck of a ship; each hall was 1700 feet long, a nice walk in itself, and there were thirteen miles in that one plant.

The shops were numbered, with around forty people in each room, clean as the parlor at home with pale green walls and ivory ceilings. All tables and machines were grounded thirty feet under the quiet earth, and all doors had copper plates on them that drew static electricity out of the workers. We were required to touch these plates as we entered or left the shop. Lights were sealed and there were no electric outlets. Also there were no windows and light was all artificial.

To my dying day I will never forget how tired I used to get,

191

especially on the night shift. We had been assigned where we were to work and someone put me on a three ton powder press. It was a huge machine; I could hardly see around it. All I had to do really, was to pull and push back a lever that would shoot an empty cartridge into position and fill it with gun powder; another shove sent it back and out to a conveyer belt where it would be carried away.

I could never understand why anyone would put a very small five foot woman on such a machine, but I stuck it out for nine months. When I finished, my left thumb was paralyzed; it stuck out straight from my hand and it was months before I could bend it; even now, thirty-five years after, it still clicks when I try to bend it.

One time I had been on the night shift for two weeks and was just plain played out. We were all getting three days off; my mind was completely at ease when I got on the Bloor streetcar, so I took a backseat, slumped over into the corner and went to sleep. That was around eight a.m.

When I didn't come home Mrs. Dawkins got worried and phoned the plant, and they said I had been cleared out. So she phoned the Toronto Transit Commission and told them her story, and asked them if they had spotted me in their streetcar. They alerted the drivers, and to make a long story short, they found me on the Spadina streetcar miles from home. But when the car got to the Spadina and Bloor end of the run, the conductor woke me and walked me over to the corner of Spadina and Bloor, pointed out my boarding house, and told me to be sure and go straight in and go to bed.

There was a fellowship among the workers. We seemed to be part of a vast cavalcade moving on to some fixed destiny, something bigger and stronger than ourselves, but in which each one played a part. We were the *Grapes of Wrath*; we were the crusaders marching toward Jerusalem; we were all the Sir Galahads of the world seeking the Holy Grail.

For we were the little people of the world, the workers, the muckers, the trail breakers. We had discovered continents, founded empires, built bridges. We had spanned the rivers of the world, laid the foundations of freedom, built the pyramids;

our weapons were the spade and mattock, the pick and shovel, and the plow.

And then we stood once more, wielders of war tools. The ring of steel on steel was in our ears, the blue glare of the welding torch in our eyes.

For we knew that we were fighting for our country just as truly as if we stood on the cliffs of Dover or roared down to drop an "egg" on a loaded barge waiting to cross the channel to England.

For there was a war on in which children were the tender targets, where the old and feeble were easy victims, where youth and love and happiness were trembling at the stakes — a war where God was mocked and goodness and mercy were heaped with scorn. Churchill said in one of his broadcasts, "I am thinking of all those women and girls who at the call of duty have left their homes to join the services or work in factory, hospital or field."

So we too were warriors of his majesty's forces, who fought on the home front, working day and night.

A little puff of powder burning out
A sharp command . . . the scuff of hurrying feet,
A red cut on a hand . . . a powder burn,
And still the work goes on . . . the hammers beat,
Their ancient litany of toil and tears,
Like a great chorus singing down the years.

We worked in unity and cheerfulness, and a strange loyalty grew up among us to each other, a protective feeling as if we belonged somehow to something bigger than ourselves.

The hours sometimes dragged with weary feet, but now and then we would sing, old favorites, new battle songs, and hymns that sounded strange in the sober setting. I remember one dreary night a young boy began to sing as if to himself, "Land of Hope and Glory". In a second, everyone in the shop was singing tunefully as if it had been rehearsed, "Mother of the Free, how shall we extoll Thee who are born of thee . . . ." The little English boy was leading, his head thrown back, his hand upraised like a choir master, "Wider still and wider shall thy bounds be set, God who made thee mighty, make Thee mightier yet . . . ."

Up to the long white ceiling the song floated, and down the glistening hallways, and now I know that however long life may last for me, I will remember the weary munition workers singing "Land of Hope and Glory", and behind it the click of steel on steel, the whine of the presses, the hammers breaking down the steel molds, and the sound of levellers tamping the powder into a shiny brass ring.

There was a huge canteen where we crowded like hungry wolves at noon hour, or at midnight on the night shift. The food was good — hot and delicious — and served by a line of smiling women, mostly Scotch, who handed it out as if they liked their job.

On Christmas Eve we had a banquet: turkey (they cooked 300), dressing and potatoes, cranberry sauce, vegetables, and the best plum pudding that I ever sank my teeth into.

We sang carols, told jokes, wished each other a Merry Christmas, toasted each other in tea and coffee, and gave each other little presents.

The manager went from table to table giving a little speech of thanks to us for our splendid work, adding quietly, "It will be necessary for some time to come."

CHAPTER 58

A Job
in Ottawa

One day Mrs. Dawkins said to me, "Say, I saw a notice in the *Star* tonight that Ottawa needs hundreds of stenographers. You have to take a civil service exam, but you can do it." So, just for the fun of it, I went and took the exams and passed with flying colors.

A few days later I got a phone call to report to Ottawa within a week. By this time I didn't want to go, but after about five calls I decided that I better give it a try. I went down to bid goodbye to my poor daughter at the hospital where she was taking her nurse's training, and to my dying day I will never forget her face when I told her. She tried so hard not to cry because I was leaving her again, but I told her that Mrs. Dawkins said that if she ever got sick she could come there and she would take care of her. That comforted both of us and made the parting easier. So down I went to Ottawa, reported for duty where I had been told to go, and was sent to a huge group of buildings called "munitions and supply."

There must have been 100 girls and women, and I was taken to a big room with dozens of stenographers who were making stencils, copying letters, going over mailing lists and doing all the dozens of things that office workers have to do.

I was set to making stencils, a job I thoroughly hated. Then someone told our boss that I could write shorthand, so I graduated from a stencil maker to a real steno with a cranky boss.

Getting a room in wartime Ottawa was a mighty hard job.

Many women, hoping to pick up a few extra dollars, listed their rooms at the Y.W.C.A. So I went there and got the address of a place I might get. I went and talked to them and they said they had a room they could let me have. There were two nice little children, and the place looked clean and was near a car line. I was to get my own breakfast and get my other meals downtown. That was fine.

I had been there about a month when, one night after I got into bed, I heard fighting and screaming downstairs, door slamming, things being thrown. There was a terrific knock at my door and the man yelled, "Is my wife in there?" When I said no, he pounded his way downstairs, found her in the garden where she was hiding behind a stump, and from what I heard, gave her a whipping. She came upstairs crying her heart out.

That finished me with them.

Then I found another room where there were two grown-up girls and an old sick mother. It looked nice and clean so I moved in. It didn't take me long to learn that the oldest girl had a boy friend who was a cabinet minister, married and with a nice family, who used to come and spend the nights with her. But she was nice to me and I thought it was none of my business. Then one night they had a screaming, hair-pulling fight too, and I was told to get out. So I packed my turkey and went room hunting again.

There was a nice woman named Mrs. Frood, a widow near my age, who worked in the same large office as I did, and one day she said to me, "Why don't you come and live with me? I'll rent you a room and you can do your own cooking." I jumped at her offer and moved in. She was kindness itself to me, and now over thirty years after, she is still one of my best friends. We still laugh over our memories and have lunch together when I visit Ottawa.

CHAPTER 59

The Alaska
Highway

I worked in the same office for about a year and then, as usual, got fed up with the dull routine of it all. I guess I was just born to be restless; it must have come from my ancestors who were mostly sailing men with the restless sea in their blood. So one day I decided that I would like to see the Alaska Highway, that 2,000 mile road that was being built from Dawson Creek to Alaska.

We all knew the Japanese were flying over the north country with the idea of coming in if the Germans ever got their feet on Canadian soil. So the Americans moved in, thousands of them, and started to widen the road north, which up to then was just a good common road for settlers coming into the Peace River country. One day the Japanese blew up the bridge on the Peace River, and that settled it.

The U.S.A. moved a huge army to Dawson Creek. They built a big camp of 10,000 men and worked from there, built smaller posts about every hundred miles. It changed the face of the country. Homesteaders got jobs trucking and made the first good money they had seen for years. Fleets of trucks started hauling supplies north and ever north; you could hardly see the road ahead of you for the dust. Farmers from Saskatchewan and Alberta came too, left their crops to take care of themselves, and made little fortunes on the road.

One day, there in the office, I got the notion that a good story was up there. I said to my boss, "I want to get out of here.

I want to see the Alaska Highway." And he shouted, "You're nuts. You can't leave here, we need you. This is a war office, you know," and walked away.

One of the men heard him and whispered to me, "Go to Paul Martin. He'll let you off for three months." So I went to him, told my story, and he thought for a minute and said, "Do you think you could do a good story on what is going on up there?" When I said yes, he wrote a note of permission; I packed my suitcase, bought a ticket and was away with other office workers shaking their heads and telling me to be careful.

When I got to Edmonton, I boarded another train for Dawson Creek. Three quarters of the passengers were soldiers, all in sleeping cars; there were only three civilians beside myself in our car. My upper berth was supposed to hold a soldier, but he got so drunk he couldn't get up. He made a dozen awkward tries, so I got mad and yelled at him, "Get up there you old fool and shut up!" He answered me in a slow Yankee drawl, "Cain't you see I'm a-trying ma'am." Then I shouted, "Shut up," so he just slept on the floor and snored all night, peaceful and quiet, with the conductor stepping over him carefully. Someone threw a blanket over him and he slept like a baby until we pulled into the station at Dawson Creek.

But getting up the Alaska Highway was a different adventure. I wanted to do my story, but how to get past the barrier was something.

The U.S.A. had put a huge sign across the road to the Peace River that said "No Trespassing" and soldiers were watching it day and night. So Dawson Creek was as far as I could go. I went into my little restaurant there, had lunch, and as I paid my bill, I said to the cashier (who was a young Chinese girl), "I wonder how I could get up the highway."

She laughed and said, "I know who you are, you spoke to our Chinese mission once in Victoria. Come with me. I'll get you across." So we went out to the curb where a mail truck was standing, and she told me to get in, get in the back, and sit on a box. So I did. When the young mailman came out he looked in and said, "How in hell did you get there?" She said, "Shut up, she's my friend and wants to get across the river." With that she gave him a shove and he said, "Oh, all right. Put that bag over your head when we get to the check point," and away we went.

We passed that one all right, then went on to the river where about fifty loaded trucks were standing, waiting their turns to cross on a huge American scow. As I said, the bridge had been blown up a few weeks before.

The mailman was waved on, and as we eased down the bank he hissed at me to keep still; under the bags piled over me, I laughed to myself and wondered what my mother would think of me now, crossing on an army scow under a pile of dirty bags.

Well, we made it and then he said, "Listen lady, I am going to drop you at the first farmhouse I come to." I said O.K. and he did. When the woman heard my name, she kissed me and said, "Come in. When did you eat last?" I was on my way.

CHAPTER 60

Return to Ottawa

From there I travelled north by army trucks and jeeps, by North West Army Command buses, and once with a load of pigs going to market. If I needed a lift I stood by the roadway; if the car had a Saskatchewan license I hailed him, and got a ride. I guess I felt more at home with a man from Saskatchewan than anyone else. One man said to me, "Gee, wait till I tell my wife that Edna Jaques rode with me for a few miles. She'll bust herself with happiness. Won't the Ladies' Aid get an earful at their next meeting."

I rode beside the truckers for miles on end, watched their knuckles whiten on the wheels, heard their breath come whistling through clenched teeth, saw them reach for cigarettes when the grade eased out, and they laughed a bit to put you off your guard so you wouldn't know how great the strain was that they drove under.

"She froze on me, lady," one trucker said, "Froze solid under me at fifty below and I thought I was a dead man for sure. But we managed to thaw her out when the sun came up, and I'll never forget how beautiful the snow glittered on them hills."

They spoke of their trucks lovingly as a man will talk about a favorite horse or even a wife. They named their trucks Maisie, Aggie, Dora or Serena. And when I heard them praising them, telling me how they handled themselves, how she purred like a kitten on a hill, I would look at Maisie and all I would see was an old battered truck with a bashed-in bumper and mud-crusted wheels; I would wonder what he saw in that mess of steel and canvas to put that look in his eyes.

And so I got my story right from the men who were living it day and night, talking to them, stopping nights when I got a chance. Some of the homesteaders up there just moved in to the highway, set up crude flop houses and lunch counters, built bunks, threw a few blankets on them, and made more money than they would in ten years on a homestead.

I hit one of those little stopping places one night about nine p.m., went to the counter and asked for a room. The man shook his head and said, "Sorry lady, I've just given out the last bunk I have." Two colored men stood by and heard him. When I said, "I wonder what I'll do?", one of the men came over with a key in his hand and said, "Here lady, we got the last one. You can have it. We all can sleep in a hay stack, but a lady has to have a room." I took the key and thanked him and all my life I'll remember this little kindly deed. And even yet long years after, I say a little word of thanks to him, when I am extra tired.

Getting back was a little miracle too. After spending about three weeks here and there in the little settlements where I spoke to some women's institutes, church groups, and a few little schools, I wanted to get back and do my story. I had been jotting down little paragraphs here and there but needed to pin it down. So what was I to do now? Somewhere up around Yellowknife I knew there was an American air base, so I headed for that.

It was about two miles out from the village, so I went out. There was a small plane loading up, and I said to the man who I thought was a pilot, "Mister, I am from Ottawa and have been doing a story on the highway. Now I want to get back to Edmonton and get a typewriter. Where are you going?" He looked puzzled for a minute and said, "Edmonton." I asked, "Will you give me a ride?" He said, "I've got a very sick man here; he is having difficulty with his breathing and I have to fly low." And I said, "Well, that's all right with me. Can I go?" He said quietly, "Get in," so I got in and away we went, flying so low that now and then we would almost brush the tree tops.

I went back a few times to sit with the sick man who was

on a stretcher, pat his hand and assure him he was all right. He would give me a little sickly smile and shut his eyes.

When we got to Edmonton, the pilot said, "Well sister, you're on your own now." I got a bus into the city, rented a typewriter at the business college and got it all down in black and white, and sent it to *Maclean's*. The title of the story was, "They Ride With Death", September 15, 1943.

A few weeks after that I was back in Toronto and riding down Bay Street on a streetcar; while we stopped for traffic, I looked out the window near a newsstand, and there I saw a big sign and the glaring letters said, "See 'Hell on the Alaska Highway' . . . with Edna Jaques." I screamed to the motorman, "Let me off," and he did; I went back, bought a copy of the magazine, sat on a box right there and read it, and decided that I had made a pretty good story of it.

Then, after a week or so resting in Toronto, I headed back to Ottawa and started working again in the Munitions and Supply Office with its stencils and lists, copying war orders, and fitted myself back into the routine with my old pals Hulda Frood, Nan Stalker and a few others. We would bring our lunches in bags, walk out at noon to a favorite high bank of the river where the beautiful Supreme Court Building now stands, and eat our lunches washed down with tea brought in thermos bottles.

Although I hated the dull routine of the office, I enjoyed these little picnics, for below us flowed the great sweep of the Ottawa River, the falls shining in the sunlight, the nice companionship of it all. One day I wrote a poem about it:

ABOVE THE OTTAWA

I love to sit at evenfall
   Beside a maple tree
And watch the mighty Ottawa
   Go marching to the sea,
Along by Hull where rapids throw
   Their snowy waters high
And pools half hidden in the rocks,
   Mirror the quiet sky.

Perchance a lonely fisherman,
　　Will lift his dripping oars,
And strike out sort of zig-zag like
　　Toward the other shore,
Or come to rest in a small cove,
　　Sheltered from wind and tide,
And set his line in quiet pools
　　Where wily pickerel hide.

I like to think that here today
　　Upon this sun warmed slope
Are still the dreams of pioneers
　　Their shining faith and hope,
Who set their faces brave and strong
　　Into a wilderness
And laid their footprints in the sod
　　To pioneer for us.

On a Sunday I usually attended the beautiful old St. Andrew's Church, where the elite of Ottawa went in their stiff silk dresses and stiff unfriendly faces. The only persons who ever spoke or smiled at me were the wife of the Chinese ambassador and Queen Juliana of Holland; maybe they felt lonely too, strangers in a strange land with half of the world fighting, and more than likely homesick for the sight of their homeland and the dear familiar things they remembered.

Although we worked for the war, it seemed strangely far away. No guns barking in the night, no sound of crunching timbers where a bomb had hit, no bread lines with women standing hours on end for the rations. It was almost unreal, as the days and months passed and the end of it still not in sight.

But the awful headlines in the papers told us the terrible news of bombing raids that laid half of cities in shambles; they told of little houses, hundreds of them, blown apart, and women sitting in groups, clutching their children with looks of horror still on their poor faces, not knowing where to turn or what to do next.

The morning after Coventry was bombed, there was hardly a word said in the offices. If anyone spoke, it was in whispers. Even in quiet Canada we felt the horror of it, as if the end of the world was near and all you could do was sit and wait.

One day a little blue letter came to me from Dorothy, the girl my mother raised who had married and gone to England, and whose husband Alf had been killed at the landing in Africa. She had had a little girl and was expecting another child when Alf died. In her letter she told me that she had gone to the hospital when her baby started to come, and that night the worst air raid ever known in Newcastle started. All night the German planes flew back and forth, throwing their awful bombs, thousands of them. They were trying to knock out the docks of Newcastle, and as the hospital was in that vicinity, they were in the thick of it.

Most of the patients were put in the cellar, but Dorothy was in labor and couldn't be moved; so they put her mattress on the floor and put a steel table over her and there Alf's son was born. He grew up to be a little fair gentleman who now lives in Winnipeg with a wife and two children, earning a modest living for them; he wouldn't say boo to a goose.

One day I was standing in that little place in front of the Chateau where a lot of the buses passed — a narrow strip that kind of united upper and lower Ottawa. There was a soldier there too, a little thin fellow whose uniform hung on him; he wasn't the usual type pictured on the posters with square shoulders and a happy grin on his face.

This boy looked barely eighteen, a gentle home boy that war had caught up with and he was still bewildered. This poem came to me, almost like a prayer:

I PRAY

Not for the brave and stalwart,
Happy behind their guns,
But the little homesick fellows,
The gentle kindly ones.

Not for the up and coming,
    Dauntless and unafraid,
But the freckled kid scarce out of his teens
    Holding the barricade.

Not for the lusty commandoes,
    In love with the game,
But the little shrinking private,
    Unknown to fame.

Not for the gay adventurer,
    Lusting for the fight,
But the stay at home from a little shop
    Facing the battle's might.

The humble, the meek, the discouraged,
    Facing the cruel day,
The boy who will never come home again,
    For THESE I pray.

CHAPTER 61

The War
Goes On

My daughter Joyce graduated in 1945 and I went to Toronto to see her. How proud I was of her, that she had stuck it out without much help from anyone, no one but me backing her and encouraging, no relative to slip a dollar to her now and then, just her own sturdy self battling with bed pans, scrubbing floors, making beds, looking after patients.

The war was still on and hundreds of girls had joined the armed forces or worked in war factories getting good money. It was almost impossible to hire a girl to work in a hospital, so the little nurses had not only to do all the work their training required of them, but hard menial jobs besides — keeping the wards clean, washing windows, scrubbing floors — and in their one-hour break trying to get their book work done. Twelve hour days sapped their strength and left them, at the end of their training, utterly played out and not fit to start in earning their living.

Joyce stuck to it, like she always did. And then one day after she finished, she met a pilot from the Trans Canada Air Line and he told her to apply for a job as stewardess. Before I knew it, there she was, pretty as a picture in her new uniform — navy blue with a little jaunty hat perched on her head — and happy as a clam.

How proud I was of her. Sometimes I managed to go out to the airport at Ottawa and have a short visit with her while the plane loaded up. As she stood on the steps of the plane checking the passengers in, I thought my heart would burst with pride; I would tell everyone around me who would listen that she was my daughter.

When Arthur Haley was doing his story, *Airport,* he spotted her and asked the chief pilot if he could use her for his pictures. The pilot said yes, and when Haley's story came out, there Joyce was, pretty as ever, serving lunch to a passenger, or standing on the steps of the plane with a couple of pilots. I thought my heart would burst again, and knew that all the hard years were over for both of us. We had finally got on our feet and please God, we may never be so hard up again.

One day I was called to the phone and a strange woman's voice was inviting me to lunch. I went and met her; she had been sent to offer me a much better job writing publicity for the War Prices and Trade Board. I refused right there. The next week the same girl called to take me to dinner, and the same offer was made. I protested that I didn't have the faintest idea of what they wanted. The next week there was another phone call, so I went over to the W.P.T.B. and met a group of men and women and made a bargain. "All right," I said, "I'll come, but if I fail I will be paid my salary to the end of the war." And they all shouted, "It's a deal."

What they really wanted was a woman to write little newsy stories coaxing women to take it easy and do all they could to help the war effort. I might say with due modestly, I succeeded beyond their dreams. Every newspaper in Canada used them, especially the papers in small towns, and farm magazines. When they showed a basketful of my clippings to Donald Gordon, he said, "Well I'll be damned. And she writes good poetry too!"

One of my assignments was a trip down to the Atlantic Coast. I was billeted in a farm house right on the shore of the Atlantic on the Bay of Chaleur; I was told to get a story about how the women of Nova Scotia felt about the prices board and the war and the rumors of German submarines nosing their way along the shores, coming in at night for fresh water from the little creeks that were so plentiful in that particular district.

So there in the kitchen of a farm house, close to the shore, I got my story, and knew it was true. There were submarines creeping in the darkness, close enough for their crews to get out and fill their tanks with fresh water, take a dip in the sea and have a good run along the beach to ease their cramped muscles, and get back before dawn to hide beneath the sea.

Everyone knew it, but was naturally afraid to do anything about it. What could they do anyway? So they just kept still, sat in their quiet kitchens with the windows darkened and doors locked and hoped for the best. As far as I know there were never any incidents, but I can tell you, sitting in a warm kitchen after supper, little shivers would chase themselves up and down my spine, while I wondered what would happen if someone would burst in the door, maybe a few of the younger men looking for excitement. I was glad when I felt I got a good story and was back in safe old Ottawa, far from the terror by night.

My boss was delighted with the story, and that was the end of it as far as I was concerned. Looking back after more than thirty years, I never heard of an ugly incident of anyone being killed by someone from a submarine whose crew had a little break, and went back to their lonely life beneath the sea.

The Wartime Prices Board was often entertained by various embassies or big business, I suppose in order to get a good story from it, or maybe they just thought we needed something to cheer us up.

One time we were invited out to Prime Minister Mackenzie King's home up near Harrison Lake. After seeing the gardens and most of the house, I got tired and found a nice little veranda at the back of the house behind the kitchen with two old rocking chairs on it. I sat down and rocked and enjoyed the scenery and the peace of the yard with its lovely overhanging trees, and the kitchen garden.

After sitting there for about fifteen minutes, a man came limping out and sat on the other rocker; when I looked at him, I realized it was the lord of the manor himself, Mackenzie King, looking fagged out, mopping his face and resting. And that is where they found us about fifteen minutes later, each rocking quietly and talking about the prairie.

Another day we were invited to a tea at the British high commissioner's place in Ottawa. After being warned not to do anything wrong, I did just that. As I came in the front door, there was a man with his hand out, whom I learned later was the high commissioner himself. I brushed his hand aside, and went farther in and shook hands with the butler who looked the most distinguished among the men then went into a corner and had a good laugh at myself and the look on his face.

Again, at a tea at the governor general's home, I got tired of the incessant chatter and laughter, and lay down on a very wide window sill and went to sleep. And that is where they found me that time. Jean Love hauled me out and said if I ever did a thing like that again she would crown me. And so the social life went on; we were somehow part of the busy and sometimes happy life in Ottawa in the war years, when the fighting and bombing seemed as far away as Mars or some remote island in the south seas of which we were hardly aware.

Donald Gordon used to sit on a little settee and play his small accordion, lovely Scotch songs that comforted him for he was homesick for Scotland to his dying day. He missed the glens and hills and the heather, and the lonely moors — and everyone liked him.

When I was working there I got out a new book of poems entitled, *Back Door Neighbors.* Then I thought it would be nice if Donald Gordon would write the foreword for it, so I wrote a few paragraphs and took it down to his office, asked his secretary, Nan, if she thought he would sign it.

She said, "I don't know, he's in a hell of a humor today; but there is only one thing I can promise you, if he throws you through that door, I'll pick you up." With that she opened the door to his office and announced primly, "Edna Jaques to see you sir."

And there he was sitting at his desk with his fists clenched and his face red with anger. He looked up and growled, "What do you want?" I told him that I wanted him to write the foreword of my book. He shouted, "You know I can't do that," and I said, "You don't have to, I have it all written. All you have to do is to sign it."

He said, "Let me see it." I handed it to him and walked away and looked out a window. He read it, cleared his throat and said quietly, "I'll be proud to sign this, and thank you for asking me." He stood up, all the anger gone, smiled and we shook hands. When the book came out I sent him a copy for his wife, Maisie, whom he so dearly loved.

One day a letter came from Joyce containing world-shaking news. She was engaged and going to be married to a Jewish friend, Murray Sugar, right away if I didn't mind. They were in love and although he still had two years of university, they thought they could make it. She would keep on with her nursing; he was taking pharmacy and could get a job any place when he got through.

I went numb all over, a cold wave swept over me. Jewish. How would a good United Church girl get along with a Jew? Would she turn or would he? As it happened, neither "turned", they just quietly stopped attending any place of worship, and as far as I know there was no quarreling and no interfering from either me or his people. We all get along fine, but I know both mothers were disappointed and sad at the turn of affairs.

They were married by a Toronto rabbi at a relative's place, then came to Ottawa by the night train, sitting up all night. She said she didn't feel married until a United Church minister said it was all right.

A western friend gave her a lovely little wedding in her own home out at Brittania Heights, and her minister performed the service right there in their living room. They both looked lovely, young and vulnerable and full of confidence in the future. We had a few western friends and five or six Ottawa friends; Florrie, my friend from Moose Jaw, put up a nice lunch and everyone went home satisfied in their hearts and hopeful that all would be well.

I had reserved a nice room for them in the Lord Elgin Hotel, and a friend, Harold Johnston from Rouleau, Saskatchewan, drove them down and thus began their married life. I went back to my routine at the office, praying that all was well with them. And I might say that now, nearly thirty years after, they are still in love and happy. He adores the ground she walks on, and she still gets a glow on her face when he walks in the door.

• • •

The day of the invasion dawned bright and clear. All had

been holding their breath, secretly, prayerfully, hardly daring to think that it would be coming soon. We knew in our hearts that it had to be before another winter set in, and that it was now or never. England just couldn't stand another winter of darkness and bombing. Even the stoutest hearts were beginning to feel the awful strain and wondered just how much longer they could hold out.

I'll never forget the day it started. I think everyone I passed on the street was praying; women walked along holding their beads as if for comfort, tears falling quietly as they shopped or went quietly about their work.

Thousands of people jammed the churches. I went to dear old St. Andrew's, and sat quietly with the rest of them, each one just sitting there, everyone praying, wiping the tears away, not saying a word. Princess Juliana of Holland was there, her nice face awash with tears, yet holding her head high as she looked up at the beautiful stained glass window with the picture of Jesus blessing the children. We all seemed one; humanity, I guess you would call it, united, in an overwhelming prayer that somehow, some way peace would come.

The next day things quieted down and we went our ways, confident and glad that surely now the end of the war was in sight like a high mountain seen through a mist.

Joyce's baby, Gary, came along in proper time, born in the same hospital she had trained in — Women's College. He was a beautiful child; he looks like his great-grandmother, Scotch as if the heather was growing out of his ears, deep blue eyes, curly brown hair, a real Scotch complexion. He is a geologist now, making more money a year than I ever saw.

Steven came next. We don't know who he looks like. He has bright red hair, brown eyes and freckles. Both boys grew to be 6' 3" tall. At fifteen, Steven was the junior skating champion of Canada — that is his forte. He teaches skating in some of the finest clubs in Toronto, and is happy with his work.

Nancy, my love, is Scotch, too, with the same deep blue eyes as Gary, lovely complexion, nice hair. If you met her on the road in Scotland, you'd never know she was four generations Canadian.

Louise takes after my mother. She is as Irish as Paddy's

pig, even talks Irish without knowing it; she is friendly and outgoing, takes life as it comes, has a hundred friends, and drives a car as if the devil were chasing her; she gets a happy kick out of life that is good to see.

I started taking Gary to Sunday school when he was two years old, and as the others got old enough they went too, all of them. The boys attended Cubs and Scouts in the Oriole York Mills United Church, and when Gary was eighteen he was elected the "Chief Boy Scout of Canada." The church gave him a banquet. The night he received his award, Murray was the guest of honor at the banquet; he sat between Gary and the preacher and his face shone with happiness. Indeed, I thought he was going to break down and bawl, and I think he was the proudest father in all of Toronto that night.

The girls went to Canadian Girls In Training until they got too old for it. Our connection with the church is still there, like a golden bond of something above creed or religion.

I still belong and believe it or not, hardly ever miss church. On my eighty-fifth birthday they gave me a lovely supper and a bouquet of flowers, with me sniffing and almost weeping with happiness that they had been so nice to me — an old woman living far beyond her alloted time, and still enjoying life, hoping to finish this book before the curtain falls.

CHAPTER 62

The War
Ends

The day the war officially ended, May 8, 1945, Ottawa went crazy. We went to work as usual, but no one did a tap, you might know. We laughed and talked and kissed each other, and then went out on the streets along with countless thousands of others, walking and laughing and singing, saying hello to strangers, looking up to the beautiful flag waving slowly in the bright sunshine above the Parliament buildings, triumphant as Britain and her colonies ruled the waves, and the skies.

A little boy about five years old came and sat down beside me, slipped his tiny hand into mine and told me he had lost his nurse and would I find her for him. I comforted him, bought him an ice cream cone and handed him over to a policeman who said, "Come on son, we'll take you home."

I remember seeing a tall dignified Englishman walking along Sparks Street without the shadow of expression on his face, just staring ahead. In his hand he held a roll of toilet paper with the ends trailing behind him, slowly unwinding. I cannot imagine why he took this freakish way of expressing his joy, but there he was as dignified and proper as if he were entering Westminster Abbey at a royal funeral.

And so the day passed, the crowds growing every hour, more and more people crowding the streets. They say the pubs were overflowing, and I bet they were. The churches were full too, jammed to the doors; people, just ordinary people like you and me, thanked God for peace, knowing now that their sons and husbands would be coming home to take up the difficult and hard job of fitting back into their old world that would never be the same for them or anyone.

After that we went to work as usual, but we all knew that our "jobs" were finished. They wouldn't need us now to send out our stories and bulletins and keep the people posted on what was going on, or what we expected them to do by way of help.

A lot of the higher-ups had been on loan from their companies, banks; they were in insurance, advertising and newspaper work. Slowly, day by day, a department would close up, and I knew my job was finished too.

Then I was offered a job with Lotta Hitschmanova; I was to travel with her and write feature stories for her campaign for homeless and poor children, in almost every part of the globe. I didn't want that.

Then I was sent for by an executive of a government department to come and see him about an offer to work in his office writing publicity for him. I didn't want that job either, but went to see him. He was a pleasant man from the west, and thought I could do a good job for him. After answering all his arguments, I thought I would cinch my refusal and said, "Look mister, I don't know what you're talking about. I only went to grade eight and I just couldn't pass the civil service test." He laughed and said, "Don't tell anyone, but I didn't pass grade eight myself." Then I told him I didn't want to stay in Ottawa anyway; I was going back to Toronto to be near my lonely daughter. And he said, "You are doing the right thing."

So I packed my small belongings and got the train the next day feeling kind of good within myself; I felt that a job had been done to the best of my ability and now I was back on my old level, scratching a living where and how I could.

How I hated to leave my friends: Hulda Frood, with whom I had lived for four years; Nan Stalker, a little widow who followed us around wherever we went and hardly said a word — a nice gentle woman, a home-body, but life had pushed her into the world and she too had to earn her living; Thelma Taschereau, one of our press room girls; Helen Beatty from Regina; Thelma Craig, a newspaper girl from Toronto; Elsa Herwig, an English woman who longed for her lovely home on the outskirts of London but hated to leave Thelma. But as my daughter said — you can't bring them with you.

There were a few men (believe it or not) that I hated to leave, big shots loaned to the government too because they were good businessmen and good organizers, and with flares for getting things done fast: Ken Taylor from Montreal, Ralph Mackay who kept the newsroom hopping, Brian Vaughan, who went back to his advertising company; there were a few others whose names I cannot remember, but I remember them kindly and wish them well.

• • •

On one of my trips to Ottawa after the war, I visited the president of the Women's Canadian Clubs. Sort of joking she said, "Why don't you take a crack at visiting some of the clubs in the States? There are hundreds of them; I can give you the name of a nice lady in Boston who has a good speakers bureau. I think you would be all right for them too." So I said, "Well, give me her name and I just think I will do that. It wouldn't cost much to go down and I've always wanted to see Boston, anyway."

So down I went, found a nice quiet little hostel for women and got in touch with Mrs. Frame, the program woman. She said, "Well you are lucky, I had a cancellation from a speaker yesterday and I can fit you in on Friday for an audition."

When I got to the big hall, there were about 200 women in the auditorium, and I was lead or pushed into a little waiting room at the back. There were about twenty-five women, all nervous as debutantes, waiting their turn to go on the platform and do their "show". Each one was given five minutes; if she didn't make it by that time she was scratched off the list.

I was terribly nervous myself, and wondered what on earth I was doing there with all those smart people. So I got a glass of water, went over into a corner and tried to tell myself that I would be all right.

About two minutes before my turn came, a woman put her arm around my shoulder and said, "You're a Canadian, aren't you?" And when I nodded "yes", she said, "Well I'm from

Kingston," then started to cry and said, "Get up those stairs, and God save the Queen!"

She saved the day for me too. I was still laughing at her when I hit the footlights, and went on from there with a couple of jokes, a tiny story and then a poem. When I finished the women started to clap. At noon I spoke to the program woman; as she put my name down she said bitterly, I thought, "Well little lady, you stole the show. I have enough dates to keep you going all next winter." When I got back to Ottawa and told my friend what had happened, she nearly had a fit laughing. I found the American women exactly like our own; they laughed in the right places, praised the same poems, and entertained me like royalty.

CHAPTER 63

A Place of
My Own

The day I "packed my turkey" and came back to Toronto was sad, in spite of the fact that I would be near Joyce and her young husband in their new house in Leaside. I felt lost, as if I were standing at a crossroad and didn't know which way to turn.

I rented a housekeeping room with a cranky old lady who bugged the daylights out of me, but rooms were hard to find at that time. I put up with her badgering for a couple of months and then let fly my Irish temper at her. I out-shouted and out-cussed her, and from that day on she was kindness itself, and we got along fine.

I wanted a bit of land. I don't know why a middle-aged woman would want a farm, but that is what I wanted; so one day I found a real estate agent at Clarkson and told him what I was looking for.

He said, "I've got the very thing you want. Let's go," and we drove out along the Lakeshore highway about ten miles, made a turn, and there it was — the place of my dreams, three acres between the highway and the lake. It was immediately opposite the big old Gooderham house, set back among the trees. In fact, it had been part of the Gooderham estate. I said to him, "I'll buy it." Just like that. A thrill of happiness washed over me, and I said to myself, "I'll plant a few apple trees, a couple of peach, a pear, some grapes, and have a nice garden; when I get my old age pension, I'll be fine, just fine." So the deal was closed, papers were signed, down payment handed over, and I wouldn't have traded places with the Czar of Russia.

I had carpenters come and put up a tiny two-room house, with a big window facing the lake; I bought some second-hand furniture from the estate of an old lady who had died recently: a nice bedroom set, a few chairs, tables, stove, and a desk for my typewriter. When the carpenters handed me the key and went away. I went into the little bedroom, got on my knees and thanked God that after almost thirty years of wandering and living in other people's houses, I could lock the door and be "home".

How I loved that little piece of land. It was rich soil; someone told me that the waste from the huge liquor vats of the distillery had been put on it. Whisky or no whisky, it was wonderful; and at that time I wouldn't have traded it for a farm in heaven.

I bought fruit trees, every kind that would grow in the country, and they shot up and spread out and became lovely trees in two years, and bore their fruit. After the treeless prairie, to have real fruit I could go out and pick was almost unbelievable. How I wished my dear mother had lived to see it and share its bounty. I would look out the window and hardly believe my eyes — that me, Edna Jaques, was growing fruit.

I put in about a half-acre of strawberries, eight long rows of raspberries, grapes with a little trellis to hold them up, asparagus, and planted a row of trees to the lake to set the boundary between me and my closest neighbor — a nice elderly Dutchman and his Canadian wife. It was a great comfort to have them so close; I knew that if I got frightened in the night, I could run over there and sleep on the couch in their front room. I only did that once — the evening of Hurricane Hazel when the wind almost took the roof off the house, and theirs also.

The second summer I rigged up a little roadside stand and sold fruit in front of the house. It was fun talking to people who stopped to buy the heaped-up boxes of berries for twenty-five cents. One day, my daughter and her husband were out picking while I sold; we tied the little two-year-old boy to a tree near me so he would be safe. He too, smiled and waved at the tourists. Another day an American couple stopped to get some fruit and the man said, "How much for the kid?" and laughed. And I said, "He's not for sale, mister." As he walked away I heard him say to his wife, "Boy, I'd give a million dollars for a little boy of my own who looked like that."

Now and then Mrs. Gooderham would set up a little table and box and sell her fruit too. One day I asked her why in heaven's name she would do it, and she laughed and said, "Well, you seem to be having such a good time, I thought I'd try it." Imagine a Gooderham with a roadside fruit stand!

CHAPTER 64

Winds of
Change

Toward fall, requests would start to come in for me to come and give little talks to the women in churches or clubs, and sometimes for their fall suppers, especially in the smaller country churches. As one woman said, "You speak our language," and I guess I did. I told them about our farm in the West, recited poems I had written of life there which seemed to hit them in the right places. One was entitled "Farm Homes". It began like this:

> I like a kitchen big enough
>   To hold a rocking chair,
> With windows looking to the sun
>   And flowers blooming there,
> I like big cupboards by the wall
>   That hold a lot of things,
> The cups hung up on little hooks,
>   A yellow bird that sings.
>
> I like to have the supper on,
>   And let it simmer slow,
> With rich brown gravy bubbling up,
>   Around the meat ... you know,
> With apple pie set out to cool,
>   And flaky homemade bread,
> With golden syrup in a bowl
>   And jelly rich and red. ...

There are more verses, but most of the poetry had a country flavor, and it appealed to most people. I remember one man said to me, "You know missus, I thought our women were crazy to have you come and tell us about your poetry, but by cracky, it was wonderful! From now on I'll never see the farm again or turn the furrows without thinking of your poems. You have given me a brand new picture of the place, and I'll be a better man because of it." What higher praise could anyone get?

But the winds of change were beginning to blow over our nice little settlement along the lake shore, and land was news.

The first place that went was the beautiful farm that the Davidsons (from the drought-stricken west) bought, just at the turn off Highway No. 2 on the lake shore — a wide fertile piece of land on a lakefront with a high bank and deep water, an ideal spot if ever there was one for big industry who would want to ship their stuff in and out by boat. The British American Oil Company Ltd. bought it, and now ships from all over the world come and load and unload their cargoes of oil, often spilling it, where it drifts in to the beaches, polluting the half-mile beach that the early settlers got so much pleasure out of.

Across the road, a Dutch family who had barely escaped the German drive into Holland, came and were so thankful and happy to be 10,000 miles from the guns and terror of war. They too sold and moved away.

Along the shoreline next to the oil company, an elderly couple had put up a tiny summer shack for weekends. That went, and I knew it was creeping toward me and my precious strip. Next went Mrs. Dutka's nice house and farm; she was Ukrainian from Dauphin where her people had settled when they came from the Ukraine, and she had known nothing but the bitterest poverty and hard work all her life. She built a tiny lunch counter in her front yard and sold hot dogs and ice cream and anything else hungry tourists called for. She was happy and talked and laughed with her customers and made nice money into the bargain; when her place went, I knew mine was doomed.

The big Gooderham farm across the road went next. The beautiful farmhouse was torn down, and she said she never passed without feeling homesick for the place where her children had been with her. Now, the big St. Lawrence cement factory is smack on the site of the old home.

One day, when I was in Toronto visiting my daughter, the phone rang and a man's voice said, "I am speaking for the St. Lawrence Cement Company. They want to buy your little farm. How much do you want for it?" I hissed at my daughter, "What'll I say? What'll I say?" And she named a price, and he said, "I'll be in to see you this afternoon." He came and the deal was made. I went around for a week in a daze, that I, Edna Jaques, wouldn't have to worry about money for the rest of my days. I couldn't believe my good luck, although I loved my white house where I could look out the window and see the blue sparkling waters of Lake Ontario stretching to the far horizon, every wave tipped with light. What would I do now? Where would I go?

CHAPTER 65

The Holy Land

After a few weeks I cooled down, and one day I said to Joyce in a timid way, "Do you know what I'd really love to do?" When she asked, "What?" I said, "Go to the Holy Land. Maw always wanted to go,but never had the ghost of a chance." But I guess some of her wistful longing came to me, and that was what I wanted more than anything I could think of. In her usual cheerful way Joyce said, "Well go!"

So that is exactly what I did. I picked out a travel agency on Bay St., and as it happened I chose the very one to help me. I went down; two or three girls were at desks and I walked over to one of them said, "Have you any nice trips to the Holy Land?" She looked startled and said, "Well what do you know, we sure have a dandy one coming up next week, and this morning, not an hour ago, I got a telegram from a woman in Seattle who was taking the trip." She said she had broken her leg and I could have her place. To this day I know God had a hand in it, not that I was glad she broke her leg, but glad I could fit into the vacancy.

It was a United Church group, forty-eight nice decent people flying together to the land of the Bible, and I knew I would fit into their company. Could anything have been more perfect? And they were leaving in a week.

I bought a new suit, a couple of dresses, a raincoat and a few other things; I walked on cloud nine during the day, and hardly slept a wink at night, and hoped that my mother in heaven knew about it.

We flew to Copenhagen first and had a day there; then there was a long eleven-hour flight to Cairo, where we stayed at a wonderful hotel right on the banks of the Nile — that great river of history where the ancient pharaohs had their palaces and slaves and wives. I could hardly believe my eyes that the wide quiet flowing river was really the Nile, with hundreds of people lying on the banks; I was told that for some of the people there, it was their only home — a ragged tent, with ragged kids playing in the hot sand, and mothers trying to make meals for them over small fires.

We visited a church that tradition said was over a cellar where the Holy Family hid while in Egypt. They told us that it was the home of a Roman nobleman and it was he who took the Holy Family in and sheltered them until the return to their own city of Nazareth.

They explained that because it was the home of a Roman lord, the soldiers who pursued Joseph and his little frightened family couldn't search the house. They would come up the narrow stone steps after dark and get a breath of fresh air, and go back to sleep on their narrow cots cut into the rock beneath the desert sand.

Early the next morning we were taken by bus about eight miles out into the desert where there was a little oasis of palm trees and a tiny spring of water, so precious in that hot country.

There we found about twenty-five or thirty camels waiting to take us the two miles to the pyramids; the camels were all lying down chewing their cuds like cows, and looking nice and quiet, which reassured us. I think the camel is the most grotesque animal on earth; surely God must have made them when He was in a mischievous mood. Instead of a nice decent back like a horse, where a person can sit, there are humps with a hollow in the middle. And, with any other animal I ever knew, their feet run back and front, to back and front; but the camel uses the two feet on the same side to do his running, making a kind of wiggly motion that is murder on a person not used to it. You just twist and turn and bounce until your poor stomach is tied in knots and the rest of your body the same, while you try to keep your teeth in, and hope for the best.

224

You get on the camel when he is still lying down; when he starts to rise you feel as if you were being dumped frontwise, and clutch the front of the queer saddle and grit your teeth, and the next thing you know you and the camel are standing safe and sound with you in the saddle.

Each rider had an Arab holding the camel on a long rope and walking ahead. I got a happy-looking fellow who laughed at me all the two-mile walk to the pyramids and back. He would shout, "Hi Ho Silver", "Ride 'em cowboy", and "Stick on bronco buster" — likely phrases he had heard other tourists shouting at each other, on other trips.

I watched our women clutching the leather wherever they could get a grip, half-scared but grim, telling themselves that this was the last straw, yet wouldn't have missed it for the world.

The pyramids fill you with a kind of frightened awe as they rise stark naked against the surrounding sands as far as you can see. Who built them, and why? Was it human labor that put those great slabs one on top of each other with hardly a crack to be seen between them? Then there are mysterious hidden passages, hundreds of them, leading into ghostly rooms; I wouldn't have taken a million dollars to go inside. How long have they stood there? Was it people from another planet with super strength who built them — or what? I wonder if it will ever be known. As everyone who looked at them was filled with wonder, and as we lined up on our camels to have our pictures taken beside them, I felt it was a kind of sacrilege to be there at all.

After our ride we were driven back to our beautiful hotel in Cairo. My window looked out toward the river (where the tiny Moses was found in his basket, hidden in the bulrushes, with his sister hiding nearby to see that he was picked up). The river looked like flowing glass as it slipped along in the mysterious darkness toward the sea, and I felt the closeness of the night as you sometimes get on the prairie in the summer when everyone on the place is asleep but yourself, and you wonder anew at the plan or purpose behind it all.

Next morning we boarded a big plane for Damascus, and

as we lifted off I felt again the sense of mystery that had been dogging me ever since we landed in Egypt.

We flew a straight line over the desert, saw the Suez Canal; how narrow and small it looked from so far up in the sky — more like a tiny creek in Ontario than one of the most important waterways in the world, cutting two continents in two, yet holding them together like a silver band.

Most of the passengers were subdued as we flew over Mount Sinai where Moses talked with God and received the Ten Commandments on a tablet of stone. How small the mountains seemed compared to our towering Rockies, how desolate and lonely and empty the desert looked where the children of Israel spent forty hot weary years before they received permission to cross the Jordan and claim their heritage.

We spent a few days at Damascus, visiting the crowded markets where you could buy anything and everything that you ever heard of. There were little stalls set off from the main runways where whole families lived, eating their meals in the open doorways — and sleeping, God knows where and how.

After Damascus we got a huge bus and started south, driving the narrow roadway along the eastern bank of the river Jordan; I don't believe there is a more desolate country in the world. Looking up toward the mountains, the scenery looked as if the end of the world had already happened. I never imagined such dark, tortured valleys as we passed — with jagged peaks shrouded with clouds, and it was here somewhere, they told us, that Jesus went alone to fight it out with the Devil, and come out triumphant over the Prince of Darkness.

We stayed the night in a lovely hotel beside the Dead Sea. Nearly everyone went bathing, but couldn't do much as the water is so salty that it bears you up. I just went wading, that was enough for me. I wiped my legs off with my handkerchief and next morning when I took it out of my purse, it was as stiff as if it had been starched. I was glad to leave that part of the country; as we drove along toward Jerusalem on the road which was nothing more than a trail, and as we passed Jericho I thought of the man who was robbed and left half-dead on the road until a good Samaritan came along, put him on his donkey and took him to the next inn and gave the innkeeper enough money to keep him there until he was well. Funny, how a little story like that could survive the centuries and still make a little glow in your heart, when you read it.

As we drove into Jerusalem I felt a queer tightening around my heart, as if I was unworthy to ride. I should have been walking, like General Allenby who walked in, not as a conqueror, but as a deliverer. I thought of the millions of feet that had followed that ancient road, through the gate; I thought of people dead for thousands of years who once had left the imprint of sandals or bare feet in the sand, refugees, conquerors, the homeless coming home, and common country people bringing their produce on their backs or on their heads to sell at the market place or in some nook set in the wall, and now tourists and Jews returning to their land, thrilled to know that for many of them, this was the end of the road and a lifelong dream come true.

Next day we went out to the Garden of Gethsemane where the trees are 2,000 years old, with gray thick bark and towering branches.

Here I wanted to be alone, to get away from voices and people, here where the tragic Jesus prayed that he might not have to go through the awful tragedy that he knew was facing him. He prayed like an ordinary human being dreading pain and torture and death — and then after his agonized prayer, told God to go ahead with it, if it was necessary to save the world and bring it back into the fold of God.

We took a side trip to the river Jordan, walked down a little hill to the river. They told us that this spot was the traditional site where Jesus was baptized by his cousin, John the Baptist. (Remember how Mary went to the mother of John the Baptist, after the angel told her she would be the mother of the savior of the world.) How natural it was that she should seek out a kindly relative to tell her worries to, and how Elizabeth too was with child.

The river Jordan is very small compared to the rivers in Canada, and it is the age-old boundary of the Holy Land. I knelt down and took a drink from the river, and a man beside me shouted, "Don't do that, you'll be dead by morning." But I just laughed at him and took another drink and nothing happened to me, and I have been glad ever since that once I drank from the holiest river in the world.

We walked to the hill called Calvary and saw an open tomb which, tradition says, was the one Jesus was laid in by his sorrowing disciples. I didn't want to look at it for some reason; maybe I thought it was too sacred for eyes to behold; a woman had her picture taken beside it and I thought she was awful.

I went around the hill called Calvary with my heart thumping, and I am sure it was the right hill. There the three crosses were raised. There Jesus hung while the Roman soldiers gambled for his garments. There the end of the bitter tragedy was enacted, and there he rose to be alive forever more.

I looked down the hill toward Jerusalem, there in the morning sunshine, past the tiny brook Cedron flowing along like a creek in Ontario, gurgling, curving around stones, flashing in the sunlight on its way to the sea, looking almost homelike where a kid could hold his little fishing rod and dream of catching a big one.

Any day you look along the roads or streets you see the little donkeys, more often than not with a woman riding, holding her baby in her arms and her husband leading it along. How familiar it looks, nothing changed in 2,000 years, Mary with her baby, and Joseph walking ahead leading it along. Somehow those little scenes, so commonplace even to this day, and the very simplicity of it, makes the story ring true.

Next day we drove out to Bethany, the home of Mary and Martha and Lazarus, where Jesus often went for peace and quiet and likely a nice meal. There in the garden we saw hollyhocks growing tall and beautiful, with a few ripened seed pods toward the top. I got eight seeds and brought them home with me, started planting them in our back yard, saving the seeds until by the third year I had a big box of them. And I wondered how I could share them with women who love hollyhocks.

One day I got the idea that maybe Lotta Dempsey of the *Toronto Star* would put a little notice in her column that I would give a few to anyone who would send me a stamped, self-addressed envelope. The response was beyond our imagination; less than a week after, I had over 1,000 letters asking for them. I put a few in each envelope. Then I ran out of seeds, and she had to put another notice in that said "no more seeds". But now I know that Mary and Martha's hollyhocks are growing in a thousand gardens in Canada, and far corners of the earth, while I still have a little patch of them in our back yard.

We visited Bethlehem, where the baby Jesus was born in a stable, likely one made of poles and chinked with mud — right where the shepherds found them and the wise men from the East came on their camels to worship, kneeling in the straw and offering their gifts. How mysterious it is to this day, how wonderful.

After this we drove to Tel Aviv, stayed a day or so and flew home. And for me, life will never the same again. I *knew* the story of the mysterious birth was true, just as it happened — the long journey from Nazareth, the crowded inn, the little stable behind the inn, the wise men, the baby Jesus sharing his first days on earth with the animals and their bed of straw.

My faithful daughter met me at the airport, her face shining out of the crowd like a light, and we drove home in the still dusk with the sun going down beyond the rim of the world. I knew I had walked on hallowed ground and breathed the clear air of the holiest city in the world.

CHAPTER 66

Thieves

After I had been home about a week I thought I would like to go out and have a look at my little house. I had rented it to two men who were working for the cement company. This company had kindly said I could leave the house there for two years until I could find a nice lot and have it moved, as they had no use for it. It was fully furnished, with a nice bedroom set upstairs, a new oil burning heater, a small frigidaire, bookcases, tables, chairs, just about everything a woman would need to be comfortable. It also had a nice sun deck at the back where you could rock and look out across the lake, see the boats passing and enjoy the sun.

So out I went, got off the bus at the right place, and could hardly believe my eyes. There was no house, nothing. Everything was gone, lock, stock and barrel. I nearly fainted. I just couldn't believe my eyes; even the cellar hole had been filled in. I walked in a daze over to my neighbor's, knocked at the back door and pointed to where the house had been.

Mrs. Erklin said, "Come in. We don't know anything about it. We heard a lot of noise one night, trucks, men cursing and yelling, and as we looked out toward morning, the house was gone. I think they loaded it on a huge truck and drove off. Isn't it awful?"

Well it sure was for me. I was in a daze for a few days and then went out again to see if I could find anyone who knew what had happened or where it went.

I went to see the St. Lawrence Cement Company and the

manager just slapped his hand on his knee and said, "We don't know anything about it," and turned back to his work.

I called the police and they came and kind of laughed. The mounted police said, "We don't know anything about it." I talked to some of the workers down by the dock where they were working and some of them snickered and said, "We don't know nothing."

And to this day, ten years later, I have never found out or spoken to anyone who could give me a clue. I think it was one of the meanest things that was ever done to an old woman, who had no one to defend her or help in any way. If I had been younger I might have put up a bigger fight and got it back.

I might say, it wasn't a shack. It was a well built lovely cottage that had cost me over $5000, and I hope the men who stole it have bad luck as long as they live.

CHAPTER 67

Another
Move

What would I do now? Where would I go? My daughter's home in Leaside was rather small — one of those semi-detached they call them. It's really two separate houses joined together, but entirely separate as far as living in them is concerned.

When I told Joyce and Murray what had happened, they couldn't believe their ears. Then, seeing how very upset I was, they kindly said, "Now mother, don't get sick over it. You can stay here with us and help with the kids. We'll fix up a little corner in the basement for you, and see what happens." Well nothing happened. I settled in with them. The youngest child, Louise, was about two, a nice happy little girl; the next one, Nancy, was two years older; the two boys were going to school and so were away most of the time. They were nice kids and we got along fine, with now and then a wave of a "spanker" like my mother used to use on us, and we didn't have much trouble.

My son-in-law had managed to buy a drugstore in the east end in a good district, and was making good money. Before we knew it he had bought another one, and a few years or so later, the third one. How he managed, at his age, to look after them all is beyond me. I think he is the smartest man I ever knew; he seems never to stop thinking or planning, whatever you like to call it. He would try and explain to Joyce and me what he was doing. We paid attention to what he was saying and tried to look intelligent, but it was far beyond either of us to understand what he was talking about. To this day, twenty-five years later, I marvel at the scope of his brains. He is now president of the drug trading for Canada, has building projects going all the time, speculates in big land deals, and with it all is quiet and kind to us all and is proud of his family.

Then they decided they needed a bigger house, so in less time than you could think about it, we were living in a beautiful sixteen-room in North Toronto, with a nice back yard for flowers and trees. Murray let me have a little corner at one end for my special flowers: a bed of Coronation geraniums that I smuggled home from England in my purse; some hollyhocks — eight seeds from the garden of Mary and Martha in Bethany, and I think they are the most beautiful hollyhocks that I have ever seen (deep rose color with a golden Star of David in the middle); ivy from Windsor Castle; oh yes, and "Flanders poppies" that I got from Nellie McClung's garden in Victoria, where they had been brought after the First World War by Colonel Woods, who didn't live long to enjoy them.

We have four bathrooms, which is wonderful, and I sometimes smile to myself thinking back to the little wooden affairs we had on the prairies, where you had to go, even at forty below.

But all in all it's a beautiful house and home — so homey and comfortable that none of the kids wants to get married and Gary is twenty-seven and Steven is twenty-five.

CHAPTER 68

My Grandchildren

After this, life just settled down to a quiet routine. It was so good to see the little girls going to school three blocks away in their clean print dresses with ribbons on their shiny curls.

The boys had a few nice friends, played hockey, skated, went to Cubs and Scouts. The girls went to Canadian Girls In Training and Sunday school, and fitted into the safe and sheltered life of any kid who has a good father and mother and a grandma to spoil them a bit.

How I loved to get the girls into their nice warm beds on a winter night, with their happy faces peeking out from the covers, and read a story from the Bible for them, see their eyes begin to close, know they were safe and sound. As Nellie McClung used to say, "Safe as if they were in God's pocket."

We read other stories too, *Anne of Green Gables, Heidi* — Nancy especially loved that one and vowed that some day she would visit the very place in Switzerland where Heidi lived with her grandfather. And to this day she says her first trip when she starts to make money is to go there.

I know just how she feels, for when we were young on the prairie I am sure I read *Little Women* a dozen times, and made the same vow. Once, when I was doing a series of lectures in New England, I went one wonderful day to see the old house where Jo and Amy lived, and all the rest of them — Meg, so prim and proper, and poor Beth who was never well, who Jo took such good care of. I also wanted to see the big house where their boyfriend Laurie lived, but someone said it had been torn down to make room for a row of cottages. As I walked through the musty rooms I could see it all just as the story said. I wanted to go up to the attic where Jo used to do her writing (just like I did), but the door was locked and the caretaker said he couldn't open it for me.

Funny, how the stories you read when you are young take such a hold on you. They are like friends that mold and often seem to be a part of your own life, as if you had helped live them.

Steven, my red-haired grandson, is 6' 3" tall, thin as a lath, with an Irish temper that we fight shy of; but on the whole he keeps it in check and has a nice personality to go with it.

Joyce used to take the kids skating three nights a week. She would get them at school and make them skate until their little legs almost buckled under them, then bring them home for supper and bed. I used to feel sorry for them, but I guess it kept them off the streets. But Steven is the only one who ever looks at a skate now.

He got so good at it that when he was fifteen he was ready to compete in the skating competition in Vancouver. So Joyce said to Murray, "Let's go out with him, and make a holiday of it. It isn't likely he will ever make it again." So they went out, got a nice motel near the rink, and watched the competition. The last night of it, when it was Steven's turn to show his skill, Murray got sick as a dog just from nerves, and had to go outside and sit behind the rink.

But Joyce stuck it out. The kids were all in a big room waiting their turn; each would then come out of a sort of chute onto the ice. Joyce said Steven soared out; he never skated as well before or since. He just seemed to be on wings, sailed out like a bronco at the Calgary Stampede, whirled around and started to do his act. She said she started to cry. And there was never the shadow of a doubt in anyone's mind but he was the winner; none of the other kids had a chance. And now at twenty-five he still skates like a spirit on the rink, light and graceful; he loves every minute he is on the ice.

Gary, the oldest son, seems to have inherited his father's brains in a different way. He is a geologist working for a big mining company, and makes more money in a year than I could

235

earn in a lifetime. And with it all he is pleasant around the house; if I bawl him out for untidiness, he just grins and picks up his scattered books and walks away.

Last summer, he and another young geologist were flown up to a little island in the high arctic, 2000 miles north of the magnetic pole, to hunt for minerals. They were set down by helicopter with heavy tents, padded sleeping bags, food, and the helicopter was to come back for them in a week. It came all right, right on the dot, but they had gathered so many mineral samples that the helicopter couldn't lift it and the two boys. So they drew lots to decide who would go and who would be left behind. Poor old Gary lost out; he held the shortest piece of the little torn paper. So he was left behind with the pilot's solemn promise that he would be back the next day for him, from Frobisher.

But that night a frozen fog descended across the arctic, blotting out all land and, as Gary explained, you just couldn't tell which way was up or down or sideways; there was just the thick fog that you could feel like ice against your skin, no visibility at all. So he put on his "survival bag", a very heavy bag that, he explained, looks like a huge garbage bag that zips up and does wonders for keeping the natural heat of the body in.

He said that the next morning a little white fox came sniffing along, not afraid. It's likely Gary was the first human being the fox had ever seen, so he was entirely unafraid of him, and would take bits of food from his hand. At night the little thing would curl up against Gary like a dog and sleep with him, and I still think to this day that God sent it to keep him company.

Four days after, Gary heard the helicopter hovering above him, and I am sure that when it landed Gary said a prayer of thanks for the sight of it coming down from the clouds, with its whirring motors and safety. They flew him home and told us to let him sleep and he would be all right.

After he got home he showed me the little bottle of "survival powder", with about an inch of powder left, and I can tell you that it was a thankful family that gathered that night for supper and to thank God for his safe return.

236

I wanted him to let me write a story about it for *Readers Digest* and he said shut up; to this day he never speaks about it.

CHAPTER 69

Women

I have always loved women. I guess it started with my mother, for after losing my little twin, she was terrified that I would go too, so she kept a loving watch over me day and night. I can remember her arms holding me on her lap, almost fearful that I would slip, as I was so very small; or maybe she thought that some of her abundant health would pass through her arms to me, and make me grow. Well, she succeeded in keeping me alive all right, but I sure didn't grow very big.

I loved my two sisters too, and in the early prairie years we had no one but each other to play with, so we clung together in a loving bond that lasted until Madge died. And now, Arlie and I, both over eighty, still have fun and happiness together whenever we visit.

Arlie moved to Portland, Oregon when she was young. She got a job in a big store there and before we knew it, she was married to a nice quiet man, Clarence Pearson, and that was about the end of her, as far as her family was concerned. She came back a few times to visit and I made two or three trips down to see her, but it was too far away and cost too much to be running very often.

She had one daughter, and by then her roots were bedded down; she is still there, after more than fifty years and makes a fine yankee and loves and feels at home in Portland. She belongs to a senior citizen group and I can hardly believe we are both senior citizens — and headed for the last roundup.

I have quite a few good friends too, and I still have a

special love for them when we meet and share old times together.

CHAPTER 70

Men

I have never really liked men; a cross father, a no-good husband, and a few more I could mention, have set me against men, and I am sorry.

But I have the greatest admiration for them. I think men are clever beyond words to say. The things they have invented all down the ages are nothing short of miraculous. I am amazed when I see a super plane so high up against the blue that you can hardly see it, but know by the vapor trail that it is up there, probably going 500 miles an hour, right on schedule, following the chart laid out for it to go to England or China or some far away little place in the jungle, and what is another miracle, landing in a tiny airfield 10,000 miles from where it started — right on time.

And the smaller planes making their daily flights across Canada, stopping en route to pick up passengers or let them off day after day, the year around, as casually as a farmer gets his four horse outfit hitched to a plow and does his daily acre of summerfallow or fall plowing — even that is wonderful.

Men are really inventors, and looking back farther through the ages, I wonder when the first man thought of making a plow, something he could hitch a horse or oxen on to turn the furrow instead of him grubbing with a bent stick, or digging with a sharp stone. How far away it seems, lost in the mists of time itself, but it was progress.

And then came the first sickle; how wonderful it must have looked to the man who invented it. I am sure he got more sheer joy out of it than Marconi when the first sound came in across the Atlantic to tell him that his invention worked, linking two continents together by wires carried below the sea.

And all the other inventions — more than you could count in a year: household helps, such as a meat grinder, an electric egg beater, a refrigerator, a washing machine, a bicycle, a go-cart for a kid.

You could make a list of thousands upon thousands, and wonder what unknown man, working maybe in a tiny workshop in the cellar or in a corner of the barn, made them.

I visited Brantford once on a speaking tour, and was billeted in a nice farmhouse near by. The morning after the meeting, my hostess said to me, "Come on out in the yard, I want to show you something." So I went out and she pointed to a huge tree with a wire running through it almost at the center. And then she told me that Alexander Graham Bell had lived on the next farm a few yards down the road, and he found a little corner in the hayloft and made himself a small workshop there, tinkering at the idea of a telephone or wire that would carry sound from one place to the other. "And right there," she said, "he strung a wire from his workshop to that tree. It was a small tree then — and at this end, my great-uncle, then a little boy, could pick it up, and the little gadget at the end of the wire." And there the two boys sent the first words ever sent along a wire, and no matter what the Americans say, the young Bell sent the first sound ever recorded on a wire to a neighbor kid right there in that yard.

CHAPTER 71

Successes

My books were going great guns. I had a letter from Western Producer Prairie Books the other day and they told me that my latest book, *The Best of Edna Jaques,* had sold 8,000 copies. When I told this at the recent Women's Press Club meeting here in Toronto, they all clapped and told me that was a record.

My books have caught on in Scotland too. The last book from Dundee, by the D. C. Thomson Company called *The Fireside Book,* compiled by David Hope, contained eight of my poems, and I almost burst with pride and happiness that I was in such good company as Fay Inchfaun, John Masefield, Edna St. Vincent Millay, John Bunyon and other popular poets. I am not boasting — I am just glad.

How I love to see my books sitting on a counter at Eaton's or Simpson's or Coles, smiling at me like a happy kid, as if to say, "Hi mum"; a warm glow comes and silently I thank God for their acceptance into the world of books. And somehow I feel that I belong to a "family", a book family that has been growing here on earth ever since the first scribe put his faltering thoughts down on a sheet of birch bark or a fold of papyrus made from a reed from the river Nile.

All told I have had twelve books published and have sold a quarter of a million copies (that is counting the two small ones that the Moose Jaw *Times Herald* got out first). And maybe — if I live to be a hundred — I will get a few more published. Western Producer Prairie Books in Saskatoon is the publisher. They have arranged to take enough poems for at least ten more books at intervals over the coming years.

CHAPTER 72

The Last Chapter

Now that I am eighty-five I find life more interesting than ever. I stand at the top of the hill and can look both ways, backward and forward, to the Great Beyond.

I can see the valleys I travelled alone, the little hills that I toiled up, the meadows where the going was easy for a short time, and then the hills again. How wonderful it is to see where you made the right turn, and the other times when you took the crooked mile, yet came out triumphant at the end.

For life is indeed a struggle. I don't know why it must be so, but the God of this world and all the other worlds willed it so, and being humans we have to take it as it comes.

I used to look at old women (when I was young) and wonder how they felt. They looked so placid sometimes; others looked mad; others just sat there without a shade of expression on their faces, as if their souls had gone somewhere else and left the old bodies sitting on a chair.

Not me. I love it. I love just sitting on a chair, rocking a bit, not having to solve any problems, or wonder what we'll have for supper, or how I'll get to church next Sunday — really not thinking at all. And in my life I have never known such peace.

I have a few nice friends, live in a beautiful city, have my little garden — and dearest and best, my family. What more could a woman wish for in her old age. I am thankful every day of my life just to have lived to what they call a ripe old age, with good eyesight, good hearing, two sturdy feet to carry me along, and an abiding peace that the world ahead will be lovely too.

I can say from the bottom of my heart, "Thank you God for the gift of life." And so I will close my book with this poem:

THANKFUL FOR WHAT

Not for the mighty world oh Lord tonight,
    Nations and kingdoms in their fearful might,
Let me be glad the kettle gently sings,
    Let me be thankful just for little things.

Thankful for simple food and supper spread
    Thankful for shelter and a warm clean bed,
For little joyful feet that gladly run
    To welcome me when my day's work is done.

Thankful for friends who share my joy and mirth,
    Glad for the warm sweet fragrance of the earth,
For golden pools of sunlight on the floor,
    For peace that bends above my cottage door.

For little friendly days that slip away
    With only meals and bed and work and play,
A rocking chair and kindly firelight,
    For little things . . . let me be glad tonight.